My Ride to a New Life

Follow your dreams Bob

M Bicard

My Ride to a New Life

©Copyright 2001 by Michelle R. Sicard

Printed by:
CSN Publishing
1959 Longs Hill Road
El Cajon, Ca 92021
1-800-636-7276

Printed in the United States of America

To Papi

Acknowledgements

This page is very important to me because this is where I can express my gratefulness to all the people who helped me to realize my dream, to feel welcome in a new country, and to write this book.

For your kindness, advise, encouragement, and friendship I thank (alphabetically) from the bottom of my heart:

In France:
All my family that I love very much. Especially my parents and grandparents for their love, kindness and tolerance.

In the U.S:
Linda Anderson, Dr. Claire Arment, Dr. Arnie Baker, "The Burning Tree" Restaurant family, Dr. Jack Harrison, Mike, Pat & Mel Hitchcock, Sandy Hughey, Roxanne Kempf, Karl Lapinska, Jackie Madruga , Gero McGuffin, Ned Overend , Sam Patterson, Patty & Ron Pratt, Davor Raos, Danny Ray, Jack Slovak, Robert Slovak, Elaine Stainton, Pat Stuart, Lee Stoddard, Robert Tucker, Mike Turgeon, Art Wester, Cal & Shirley Williamson.

Thanks also to the California Highway Patrol man who made me turn around on the freeway and go back to the Boulevard Exit.

And a grateful and special thank you to Katiana Raos, who has restrained her competent editorial talent to leave the French flavor intact, but made the story readable.

In Bikeland:
Sam, my two-wheeled bestfriend, for his moral and especially, his physical support!

And finally, for his patience, assistance, and love, my beloved husband Ralph.

Contents

I   Slave of Routine   9

II   The Adventure Begins   17

III   All Aboard!   25

IV   Inside Passage   33

V   What Bicycle-Touring Is About!   47

VI   Let's Try South   60

VII   Timing Is Everything   75

VIII   The Garage of Hell   100

IX   Rendezvous with Destiny   119

X   My Road to Happiness   141

    Everything Happens for the Best   159

    Postscript   159

    Letter to the Readers   160

    Contact me   160

Preface

WARNING!

THIS BOOK CAN BE HAZARDOUS TO YOUR GRAMMAR

Bonjour! My name is Michelle. I was born in 1966 in France. I grew up in Carignan, a village near Bordeaux. I have been a secretary during almost ten years. I never write before and never think I will or could. However, the last four years of my life are so incredible but true that I want to share them with you.

This story is what happened to me. All the events are true.

I am expressing myself in English for about four years. I chose to tell this story with my words. I could have used a ghostwriter or have asked someone to rewrite the text in perfect English, but then it would not have been true. It would not have been me. It would have removed the real essence of this adventure. This is why you are going to read a book with a French accent.

I hope that you enjoy this true story as much as I have enjoyed living it and writing about it.

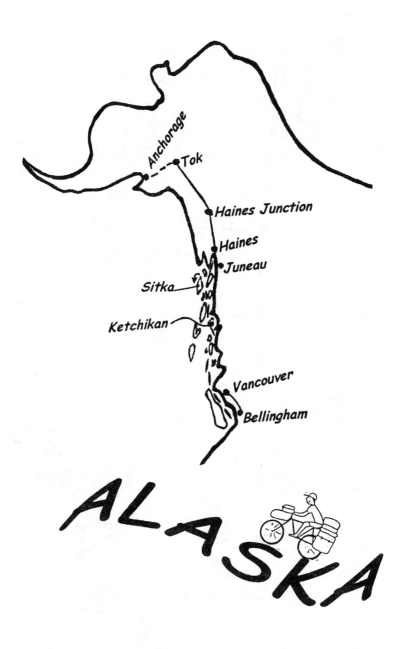

Anchorage

Tok

Haines Junction

Haines

Juneau

Sitka

Ketchikan

Vancouver

Bellingham

ALASKA

SOUTHWEST USA

I

Slave of Routine

About four years ago, I decided to stop the train of my life. I went on this train of daily routine without asking any questions, with a second-class ticket and without even knowing about first-class. But I was lucky enough to access this train when some people have to walk along the rails. To be clearer, I was born in a country and in a family that allows me an education, a job, a house, and nice friends. Everything will surely purr all my life. Who would dare complain? Certainly not me...

However, one day all this routine became intolerable. Like a costume that seemed to fit so well until today, I suddenly cramp for room. I suffocate. I must tear this fabric into pieces, break this mold that my education, my culture, and modern society has created. Of course, it is so easy and so secure to not ask too many questions, to do like everyone else, to do what this "everyone" expects from me. But here comes a day, in fact, rather a night, where revolt is stronger than reason.

The shutters are closed. The house is completely dark. I am lying in my bed. I can hear the rain outside. The temperature in the bedroom is low for the night, but I am hot. I am agitated and cannot sleep. I keep hearing in my head, "I have to do something, something that *I* choose, something that *I* want." I am turning and turning between the sheets, then for a while I am flat on my back. I am looking straight above me in the dark at the invisible ceiling. I turn my head to the side and I look at the invisible walls.

I smile thinking, "I need freedom—not walls, ceilings, closed doors, structures, schedules."

Sometimes the more difficult is to ask the right question to get the right answer. So, I ask myself, "What do you really want?" It seems so simple, "What do you really want?" Everybody has an answer. A little voice maybe so shy that you cannot hear it, or kept so deep inside for years that you forgot about it, or kept quiet because it is so weird, so impossible, so silly, so... I am sure that you know what I mean. Anyway, my voice tells me tonight loud and clear that I want to travel.

I smile in the dark. I smile because it makes me so happy just thinking about travel. I smile because the answer is so obvious. I smile because it is the truth. I smile because it is a dream.

I remember the beginning of my "traveling education," as a teenager when my grandparents took me on some short organized tours in France. Then I organized my own trips across Europe and the U.S.A. with my parents, sister, and cousins. I had so much fun studying maps for hours, planning every detail. What a joy to imagine places, read, and dream about them, then a few months later, being there. I just love it...

With a nervous move I go back on my side. I close my eyes and again feel guilty to not be satisfied. In France we are lucky to have five weeks of vacation each year, so I travel every year for about a month. With a deep sigh I think, "You spoiled girl, can't you enjoy what you have?" I feel the exterior pressures from my family, friends, work, and safety of habits erasing my dream and pushing me back in my correct and reasonable normal routine.

A new nervous move of impatience and I am again on my back. I reopen my eyes and the dream reappears, bringing me peace for the rest of the night.

The next day and the rest of the week I struggle between, "Move your butt, be brave," and "Enjoy what you have, be content." I am thinking (asking my own questions and answering) "Michelle, if you are not happy, stop complaining and do something about it." "Yes, of course, ...but what?" "Stop finding excuses—find solutions."

I try to find answers talking with friends and colleagues. They agree that routine can be boring but *"c'est la vie!"* (such is life!) They live with it, so I have to do the same. Of course, they dream to change their job, to create their own business, to try something new, to go back to school, etc. But the children, the family, the economic problems, the time do not allow them to go forward...right now. One day... later...maybe...if...when they will retire...

I listen to them and suffocate. No! I do not want to be like that. I do not want to live like that. No more excuses. "If you want, you can" as we say in France. Oh yes, I want! I really want to dare something before my excuse is, "I am too old." Here is another bad excuse. There is no age to change one's life. It is only a question of *will* and *passion.*

In this same special week, Saturday afternoon, I try to relax my boiling, confused mind and go to see the movie "Forrest Gump." It is creative, moving, entertaining, and it touched me more than I thought at first.

The next morning I go for my Sunday morning run. For the past five years I almost never failed to run ten kilometers every Sunday. During the week I try to jog about four kilometers every other day. I am going to add here that I began to run to improve my health, hoping that I would lose my twenty-two extra pounds. In fact, I quickly lose nine pounds and that's all. Anyway... I am running for about twenty-five minutes when I am invaded by an intense feeling. Thinking about the movie and the symbolism of this simple, sweet, naive Forrest Gump running across the U.S.A. brings tears in my eyes. I realize that *I can do it too.* I can travel by myself if I want. Why not? Because I thought until this very minute that a girl cannot travel alone. It was wrong. I can do it too. I need to do it. Why did I wait so long? I run harder. It is like an explosion of joy, hope, and freedom. Now I know what I want. Great! I want to travel. Fine! But how? When? Where? Answering my questions is a big step, but it is just a start. Now I have to plan my dream or risk a nightmare.

Obviously a woman alone has more chance to get in trouble, so I do not advise girls to rush forward by themselves to some crazy adventures without thinking, but to organize their projects with good intelligence. In fact I believe sincerely that everybody can do exactly what he or she wants, if she or he has the real will (the will that comes from deep, very deep inside), and a reasonable amount of common sense. In my opinion, with this recipe, all ideas are "do-able". I specify "real will" because it is easy to mistake it with a fit of temper, a period of fatigue, or the deal of the century. Very often anger, stress, loneliness, and negative feelings are factors of the desire to change life. We must use them to build something solid. No ignorant impulsion.

In my case I was not feeling good in this life apparently so perfect. By ignorance and by fear, because the unknown always scares us, I looked for excuses to keep properly the seat that society gave me. However, when it comes from very deep inside, you cannot help it and a small event like a movie can have big consequences.

This rainy Sunday afternoon is perfect for studying the situation. First, let's count the money. After a budget for food and campground, let's see what I can do about the transport. Hum...I cannot afford several airplane tickets... neither renting cars... What about buses?... It is cheaper but still too much. Hitchhiking is out of the question. Not discouraged at all, I calculate that I can walk from Bordeaux (France) to North Cap (Norway) and come back in...ONE YEEEAR!!! My brain is boiling. It must have a solution...

Suddenly I remember watching, three years ago, a slide show about a young man who travels around the world on his bicycle. Voila! There it is. Tomorrow I begin bicycle training.

From that very moment, I begin to think differently. The focus is training and organizing my project. All the things that disturb and hurt me, like stupidity, ignorance, spitefulness, hypocrisy, vulgarity, indifference, jealousy, etc...just vanish from my life. Not because they disappear from Earth, but because I do not focus on them like before. They do not touch me anymore. I feel above all this. It is wonderful to feel free and light in my own head. I feel no concern about the horrible things exposed on television or about the complaints of others. On the contrary, I find the good side of the situation and I try to communicate it. As I explain above, I use this explosion of crazy enthusiasm to organize a considered project.

It is very funny to see the look of people thinking, "She is nuts!" Funny to hear them enumerate all the dangers and catastrophes I am going to confront. Some which I even did not think about—and frankly I do not need any help to imagine troubles. I am happy, not crazy!

From this magic Sunday I use every opportunity to bike everywhere: work, shopping, visiting family and friends, plus about one-hundred and thirty miles a week of pure training. It is hard at first, but always fun because it is feeding my dream. It is part of it.

During the first months I train—crazy but true—on my one-speed child bike, and then on my grandfather's road bike, which pleases me very well. The more I study the question (in books or by talking with some knowledgeable cyclists), the more I understand that I need a better bike. After months of research, I consider to have built just for me, a special bike for my special trip. Unfortunately it cost almost my total budget. So for Christmas I decide to give myself a brand new hybrid bike. It is between a mountain bike for the robustness and a road bike for the comfort, and aluminum for the lightness. All this for a price which fits my budget much better.

Then, comes the problem of a saddle. My God, how can a bicycle be so uncomfortable for women? I almost want to say that it is a real pain in the "----" but I guess it is not a literary style! During my adventure, I am sure to not find a place to wash and dry typical cyclist shorts every evening. Since I prefer normal shorts anyway, the choice of the saddle is very important. After trying all the kinds of feminine saddles, I finally decide to keep my childhood saddle—the only one I have used and which has exactly my "shape." So, with the ingenuity and a fit of strength of my father, a professional craftsman, we install the old saddle on my shiny, brand new bike—still surprised that we can impose on it this "old thing."

When I feel comfortable enough to stay several hours on my bike without too much fatigue, I ask my boss for seven months sabbatical. Another good thing in France is that I can take as much as eleven sabbatical months. I am obviously not paid during my absence, but I will get my job back, or an equivalent, when I return. I chose seven months because it is what my budget allows me and because even if I am sure of my decision, I do not know if I can do it. But if I do not try, I will never know. And I want to know if I am right to want to change my life.

Waiting for the decision of my company, I study first, in complete euphoria, a trip across Europe. I will put my bike in the Transiberian train to cross ex-USSR, then Asia, Indonesia, and Australia! But the lack of money, time, the complexity of formality, vaccines, and a wise return to reality oblige me to change my itinerary. After a lot of research and thinking, I decide to bike across Alaska, Canada, and the United States to Albuquerque, about 6,000 miles. I choose this because I already visited three times North America. I know I will find all the gorgeous, immense, extraordinary scenic views that I like so much.

And I will stay in "civilized" country. For my first experience by myself on bicycle, I think it is wise.

I train for months. Neither the rain, nor the wind, nor the cold stops my training. On a rainy afternoon in July, before going for a ride, I stop at my parents' home. I lift up the saddle with my right hand and move the pedals with my left foot to put my bike in balance against the porch's step. Ouch! I feel a pain in my lower back. Boy, it is hurting! I come in, speak to my mother for a few minutes while rubbing my back, and then remount my bike for a forty-five mile ride against rain and wind. You need a real passion to do crazy things like that!

I ride with a light pain which hurts more when I climb; nevertheless I go on until the lunch-stop. Here I need five long minutes before finding a way to get off the bike. I even think to eat my sandwich on it. With painful efforts, I finally slide from the bike, and I walk bent at a ninety-degree angle. I try not to think about the pain as I eat my lunch on my knees. The rain is pouring harder. My back is killing me. I get on the bike again with a lot of difficulty. But she is stubborn this "cyclomaniac," and instead of going back home, she finishes her forty-five mile goal. Back in my village, I stop again at my parents' house. Looking at the floor, I say to my mother that I have a problem with my back. I go home to take some rest. Gritting my teeth, I arrive at my house and fall on the sofa... O.K. "fall" is an exaggeration; in fact, I lie down very slowly, wincing. When I wake up two hours later and try to move, it is just horrible. I move inch by inch, slide from the sofa and creep six feet in fifteen minutes to the bathroom. For a girl who wants to cross the U.S.A. in six months, it is not looking good! Then in the bathroom, I cannot reach the medicine box and stay with my nose in the bath rug until my worried mother comes to check on me...half an hour later.

During the following two weeks I stay in bed with a daily injection in the derriere. Ouch! But the worst is the thought that I might have to give up my project. It is over: Michelle biking free as a bird, taking time to appreciate life, living day by day on her own rhythm. It is a real nightmare. The dream is over.

A few days later, my back has improved a lot. I recovered also my physical and mental abilities. At the end of the second week I say to myself, "No, nothing will stop me!"

II

The Adventure Begins

During the preparation of this project I hear so many warnings, criticisms, and doubts from my entourage. I am often asked the two same questions.

The first question is, "How could you bike all these miles?" I answer that in spite of my inexperience about bike touring, my goal is to follow my own rhythm, stopping every time I need to rest. No race. No hurry. I will accumulate mile after mile, I hope without too much fatigue. I will just keep in mind the appreciation of my freedom. If it is too hard to climb sometimes, I will walk and push the bike.

The second question is, "Are you not afraid to travel by yourself?" I answer that no, I am not afraid, and no, I am not alone. I am not afraid because I organize my trip to the best of my abilities. Because I do not intend to look for trouble. Because I sincerely believe that if you do anything with negative thinking, you will attract negative events. And because I think, maybe naively, that there are more "civilized human beings" than "dangerous idiots."

About the unexpected troubles, I will have to use my common sense and deal with intelligence to make the best of it. Then, find the good side of each situation to not make the same mistake twice and in this way evolve and improve.

About traveling by myself, it is amazing, because after years of "pushing" my family members or friends to travel with me, I convinced myself that on the contrary, I must do this alone. It is my challenge—to learn to know me, to depend just on me, to find confidence.

Finally, with the risk of sounding really crazy, I will tell you that I never felt lonely when alone. I speak to myself in my head and my little voice gives good advice and serves me well until now. It is a real force for me. And I am using the light side of this force which is will, and optimism. On the contrary, if I use the dark side, it will drive me to selfishness and real loneliness.

Let's stop the philosophy and let's say that I will not be totally alone during this adventure because my bike will be with me!

In January 1996, I receive a letter from my company with my "freedom authorization." I just cry and laugh at the same time. Seven months of freedom...now I cannot go back. I have always been a spectator of my life, now I am an actor. In forty-two days: action!

In a complete euphoria, mixed with fear, doubt and exaltation, I finish my last working days. I say good bye to my surprised family and friends. They thought I would not do it. They thought that it was just crazy impulsion, that I would quit.

I train harder and tune up the organization of my trip and things. My grandparents help me to balance the weight of the luggage and gears on the bike.

Two days before the "D" day, I go to my best girlfriend's wedding. What perfect timing to leave by celebrating her love and my departure to freedom. I enjoy the party until 5:00 a.m., and one hour later I am trying to sleep in my parent's car. They drive Sam and me to Paris' Charles de Gaulle Airport. I call my bike Sam because it is the name of the hero of my latest favorite American television series.

In the afternoon we stop at a motel near the airport and I spend my last evening with my parents before the big departure. I am sure they are worried and confused but they are extremely nice and understanding. I really want to thank them for their help and support when they realized that I will not change my mind.

The 29 April 1996 I am finally in a plane flying to Vancouver, with stops in Detroit and Seattle. My bike is in a big box and I have just one fear...or two: losing the box or finding Sam in pieces.

During the flight I try to relax and appreciate, but I am so excited that I spend my time looking at maps and information about Vancouver. Where am I going to spend the night? And how am I going to cross the Fraser River? It seems that all the closest bridges are allowing just cars... I will see at that moment. I will pedal where I need to, no matter what. I try to sleep without success.

Our flight arrives late in Seattle. I have to run to get on the Vancouver plane. The flight attendant at the gate is waiting for me to board so she can close the door. Pfff, just in time! I sit down in a Dash 8, a little plane with about 20 seats. The people seem to be more in the evening bus coming back home than in a plane.

Out of breath, I fasten my seat belt. I am worried that Sam did not make it. I look out the window and see two big guys carrying my wide box. I am so relieved to see it, but I wonder how they are going to find room in this small plane which is already crowded.

We finally land in Vancouver Airport. It is 7:00 p.m. I have had no sleep for almost two days, but I am as happy as I can be. People look at me friendly. They do not seem too surprised to see this young person—girl or boy?—fighting to remove the tape and paper which protected Sam. Then putting straight the handle bar, reinstalling pedals, mirror, light, saddlebags, and blowing up the tires. They can wonder about girl or boy, because in the care to avoid troubles about my sex, and to be as incognito as possible, I had cut my hair very short, crammed my cap on my head to my eyes, and was wearing a really anti-sexy jogging suit!

Now people can see me on my knees with greasy hands, and all around me on the floor are a ton of pieces of paper and used tape, all my bicycle tools, a bag of clothes, a first-aid box, kitchen tools, a gas ring, a tent, a sleeping-bag, a camera and accessories, food cans, and diverse little things! It is a mess in the airport for one and a half-hours.

After some irritation because of the fatigue and ten hours time difference, I can finally push my one hundred pound bicycle. I know that the weight is crazy, but I did not realize it...yet!

Just ten feet further and already two people have asked me where I am going like this. After they give me encouragement, I feel ashamed to have been cranky. These friendly people remind me that my dream is beginning. My joy and appetite for adventure come back stronger. I must decide if I go outside and fight the night and the traffic of the town. I am looking at my map when a young man, who seems in a hurry, stops to tell me the way to the youth hostel, and then goes on his way. I say, "Thank you, sir...," but he is already gone.

I go outside. It is cold and dark. I decide to stay at the airport for the night. I find a small corner near the toilet (on one hand it can be practical). I put my sleeping bag on the trash bags that I packed to protect my baggage from rain, and I try to rest a little bit. Between the airport's noises, the door of the lady's bathroom, my legs folded because there is not enough room, and finally the cleaning night shift, it is another night without sleep.

At 6:00 a.m. the next morning, my adventure is really beginning. From now on, the goal of my life is to take the time to live, enjoy every minute, and find a safe place to sleep. The airport doors slide open and here I am in the real world.

I ask a policeman the way to pass on bicycle over the Fraser River. He gives me all the information and tells me that to go out of the airport area, I need to keep left before going to the first ramp. So, I get on my bike and the policeman watches me trembling and zigzagging because of the weight and the emotion of the moment.

After five minutes I feel good and so happy. Like a fish in the water, a bird in the sky, a lizard in the sun, a...I guess you understand the idea! After a few miles I can see the ramp I need to take. Like an obedient girl, as the policeman told me, I keep left. It is now 7:30 a.m. The traffic is dense. Maybe this nice policeman forgot that I am a cyclist or I did not understand what he meant, but I find myself in the middle of four lanes of traffic with no possibility to go right or left. The worst is the surprise of the motorists who honk at me and make me understand, quite rightly, to get out of their way! With sweat on my brow and my heart beating hard, I finally reach the end of this hell and take a quiet road. As we say in French: OUF! Translation: What a relief!

I bike now along the Fraser River. What a contrast! This road is so calm and has a wonderful smell of resin floating in the air. I stop to watch these big trunks of trees floating on the river. Here, everything is about wood. I pass in front of sawmills and wood warehouses all the morning. I take many detours to keep on calm roads, where I see big fields of truck farming with Asiatic workers and their typical cone shaped hats. Then I have to take a high traffic route. It is not bad actually, and not boring. I see some squirrels rushing up electric poles and wild geese in marshland along the road. After thirty-seven miles and two stiff hills where I have difficulty to push Sam, I stop at a campground. I install my camp, take a shower, go shopping, eat, and just fall into a well-deserved sleep at 8:00 p.m.

I wake up fully rested and ready for some action. I eat a quick breakfast inside, then open the tent. It is dark and rainy. What's going on here? What?! My watch shows 3:00 a.m. Oh boy! I am jet lagged! I go back to sleep with the hope that the rain will stop before daylight because closing a wet tent in its bag and letting it "marinate" all day is not a pleasant prospect for the next night. You can imagine the smell and the cold, damp ambiance—yech! Of course I know the rainy reputation of this area, so I will have to deal with the situation no matter what. Let us just hope.

I wake up again two hours later and enjoy another breakfast outside with no rain. It is so lucky. I take my time...so much time that when the rain comes back suddenly, I am not ready—not ready at all. So, it is the panic. I did not think to practice the bike organization. It takes me two hours, yes TWO, before being ready. It is a good lesson: do not waste any time before striking camp especially with the threat of bad weather.

I arrive at the Canadian/American border quite fast, easily, and with the sun. From now on, truthfully, the sun will be there everyday. I stop at a British Columbia gift shop. I am a tourist, you know. Then I try to find the way to the U.S. border when a nice Canadian agent escorts me kindly to the frontier. He even offers to take a picture of me on my "mount."

I am now biking along the Strait of Georgia in Washington State on my way to Bellingham, surrounded by multicolored azaleas and rhododendrons. It is gorgeous. I cross some beautiful countryside with mountains in the background. It is so neat to tour on bicycle! Here the roads are easy, except for some light uphills that make me worried about the next "real" ones! But I decide to focus on the present and not on the future. Good resolution girl!

Every time I need to ask my way, people are friendly, smiling, and helpful. Some motorists give me encouragement when they pass me with their cars. It is so comforting to receive this kind of support.

After a couple of hours against the wind, I arrive at Bellingham in the middle of the afternoon. I admire these beautiful houses facing the bay of Bellingham. Suddenly my eyes see something so awesome that I brake *hard*, leaving a tire imprint on the road! O.K. I exaggerate...but only about the imprint! I do stop and back up to admire closely this very pretty little house with grass so green, with azaleas and rhododendrons so colorful, and with such magnificent trees that it looks like the garden of heaven.

I go on two more hours. The town behind me disappears. I am getting tired and worried that I have taken a wrong direction. Just when I am ready to go back, I read with relief a sign saying: "Larrabee State Park." Larrabee is situated on the seaward side of Chuckanut Mountain. I am so happy to install my camp and enjoy the park. I go down on the beach.

Facing me is Samish Bay. The forest grows until the edge of sandstone cliffs, eroded by the sea. I walk to a beach and sit down on one of the tree trunks on the sand, relishing a well-deserved rest and a delightful feeling of plenitude.

I stay two days in Larrabee Park because I am waiting for the ferry to Ketchikan, Alaska. The first day I go back to Bellingham, leaving all my stuff at camp. What a pleasure to bike without any load and going downhill; I feel like I am flying above the road!

I decided to come early in the season because I read that there are a lot of flies and mosquitoes in Alaska in summer. They are also so many tourists that you need reservations months in advance. When I walk inside the building of Alaska Marine Highway, there is nobody between the cashier and me. I can buy my ferry-pass to Alaska without any difficulty.

After some shopping I come back "home" and spend the afternoon writing in my diary, writing letters, and taking pictures of the sunset. The only sound is the sea flow and the scream of the sea gulls.

The next morning I go hiking to a lake named Fragrance. I leave Sam at the trailhead. Here I learn all the nuances of the color green. I do not have a large enough vocabulary to describe it. It is the magic of the rain forest. I walk in this fascinating environment. Nobody anywhere. Suddenly I stop. Something is wrong. I do not know what it is, but something disturbs me. I wait... I listen... Nothing. I go on, and then stop again. Then I realize it is so incredibly quiet and peaceful that the sound of my own footsteps makes a horrible noise! It is like running with boots in a cathedral.

The trail stops in front of a beautiful green lake. I am not surprised by the color! I sit down on a little bench for a long time to enjoy this place that breathes peace. The only thing that breaks the deep silence is the flight of a humming bird—amazing little bird. I learn later that its wings go eighty beats a second; that is four thousand eight hundred beats a minute. What an incredible natural machine!

I come back to the campground, load Sam, and bike to Bellingham for the last time.

III

All Aboard!

One hour before going aboard the ferry, I am waiting with Sam at my side. I see a young man waiting with his bike too. We look at each other, smiling, like recognizing someone from the family—the bicycle family.

All aboard! I enter voluntarily into the wide-open mouth of a huge ferry. I attach Sam to a pipe against a wall on the car deck. Then I go up to put my sleeping bag on a lawn chair in the Solarium, which is the open deck at the back of the boat. I start to explore the boat and meet again with the young man from earlier. He smiles and asks me if I want to dine with him. I accept gladly. He speaks French Canadian. I ask him to correct me and help me with my poor English. His name is Rob. He is a student of marine biology on his way to visit his sister in Skagway. He takes his bike with him for his vacation. He is curious to know the purpose of my heavily loaded bike. We talk about my trip and many other subjects. After dinner we go back to the Solarium. It is better than a dream. The air is so cool and pure. A wonderful full moon is reflecting its brightness on this dark blue sea like a trail of light.

I learn about American tradition following Rob. We meet so many different people. It is not my nature to speak to strangers. In France the communication system is totally different. Here, people just simply come up to you, introduce themselves by giving you their first name and you feel like you are an old friend. It is interesting for me to immediately call a stranger by his first name. In France

I know some people well for years, but still never call them by their first names.

Some people are very special. We listen to an old sailor who looks like Ernest Hemingway who tells Rob and me stories about whale hunting. Later we chat with a young man with long blond hair and bare feet. He is coming to Alaska to find some work for the summer. He is taking life as it comes and enjoys it. Peace and love!

It is getting late. Everybody goes to sleep on his lawn chair. I am taking a deep breath of the cool and pure air. There are electric heaters attached to the ceiling above the chairs. It is really comfortable. What a great day! What a great night!

The next day I meet adventurers trying their luck in Alaska. Also some tourists from America and one from Australia, who give me their addresses in case I pass through their towns. A ranger woman invites me to Exit Glacier in Kenai Peninsula. A weird man who looks like a hermit tells me about beautiful, isolated places that nobody knows about. From his face, covered by a thick beard, I can only see his faraway look of happiness when he describes "his" mountains to me.

We are all confined on this boat for seventy hours. The only thing to do is relax, enjoy the countryside, and communicate a few minutes or hours with people you are never going to see again. There is no stress, no clock. We can take time.

After a simple lunch at the cafeteria, I sit down on a chair to relax and admire the natural living poster in front of me. The temperature is pleasant and the sun is shining. We are sailing in a corridor between the Coast Mountains on the east side and the Alexander Archipelago on the west side. The boat zigzags through a maze of mountainous islands, each completely covered by the forests that touch the sea. Much of Southeast Alaska lies in the Tongass Forest, which covers sixteen million acres. The warm ocean currents give this region the mildest climate in Alaska. Right now the weather is just marvelous. From time to time a narrow, flat band of white clouds seems to cut the mountains into two pieces. I feel so peaceful and happy to be here.

Lost in my thoughts, I am suddenly "awakened" by the foghorn of the boat. I stand up quickly, wondering what's going on. I lean on the rail with my elbows to see a small village squeezed between the forest behind and the sea in front. How can people live here, lost in the middle of nowhere? The only possibility to go somewhere else is by boat or plane. Then like floating in the air, I hear whistling. Wondering where it comes from, I realize that it is children running from everywhere to the bank. They know that we cannot hear their voices, so they whistle in answer to the pipe of the boat, and wave their hands. It is magic to hear the sounds of these young children celebrating our big ferry passing through. Their life style must be so different than the children in France. I am appreciative to have the opportunity to travel and see other ways to live. Little by little the whistling diminishes until it disappears.

At 5:30 a.m. we arrive at Ketchikan. It is my first stop. I put my bike against a wall of the wharf to check Sam and my stuff. Further, I notice two men who disembarked here also. They seem to be waiting for something. I am almost ready to go visit the area when the men come up to me. One is a big, rough man, who looks like a "hobo." I remember talking with him for a few minutes onboard. The other is a good-looking young man wearing clean, nice clothes and a brand new, huge backpack with a gun on the top. His style attracted my thoughts when I saw him earlier on the ferry, and I wondered what his story was. But now, he wants to know about mine. So I tell him that I am going to visit Ketchikan and some fjords.

"Do you know somebody here?" he asks me.

He is very surprised and amazed about my negative answer and about my bike trip by myself. The "hobo" smiles and goes away without a word. I keep preparing my bike with the young man still beside me.

"And you, why are you here?" I ask him.

"I always wanted to try my luck in Alaska, and I love hunting. I am Rick, Rick of Arizona."

"Nice to meet you Rick, I am Michelle, er...Michelle of Bordeaux...France."

I am ready to leave. We wish each other good luck and I bike away. The town of Ketchikan grew around salmon canneries and sawmills. Today, its main industries are fishing, timber, and tourism. I leave Sam to walk on the famous Creek Street. It is remarkably pretty and photogenic. The little wooden houses are all different shapes and colors. In fact, it is not so much a street as a boardwalk built on pilings. In 1903 the town was "cleaned" by regrouping all the brothels along the river. This was the famed red-light district in Ketchikan until prostitution became illegal in 1954. The joke was "Ketchikan was the only place where men and salmon went up the river to spawn!"

After walking across Thomas Basin, one of the three boat harbors in the city, I decide to go find a site in one of the campgrounds around Ward Lake, which is five miles north. I pass the limit of the town and a huge pulp mill. Then the road goes on across the Tongass Forest. Near Ward Lake, I find a campground with only four sites. One is available! On the left-hand side, I see a tent and a bike. The young "owner" does not seem friendly. He looks at me with no words, no smile. On the right the site is occupied, but nobody is here at the moment. I set my fabric home and go for a walk around the lake. I follow the path through the fascinating Tongass Forest. The ground is covered by luxurious new vegetation trying to hide old trunks, stumps, roots, and tangled branches.

The tremendous difference between a ferryboat full of friendly people in this vacation ambiance, sharing with others the beauty of the scenery and then suddenly biking alone, made me feel very lonely. But, after this interesting, easy walk in the nature and the sun, I am in a good mood again.

I come back to the tent and begin to cook my dinner. I install my old gas-stove and boil some water for pasta. My meals are mostly the same everyday. Breakfasts consist of a cup of dry muesli, and some very hot coffee since it is so cold in the early morning. Lunches are composed of a can of tuna mixed with some tomatoes (if I am lucky) and potato chips, which naturally, are broken in pieces by the extreme condition of transport! And for every dinner, I fix pasta with...water. It is not the sophisticated French cuisine that you might expect. The menu is driven by practicality: easy to find, carry, and fix.

While the water is trying to boil, I decide to light a fire up because I am getting cold. I do not have a lot of practice, but after a few minutes I am getting some timid flames. At the same time the "owner" of the site on the right arrives in his van. Just one man. The thought of some trouble crosses my mind for a second. I try to stay discreet. He stops his engine, and a minute later I hear him coming up to me. He has plenty of beer packaging in his hands for my fire. He says, "Hi, let me help you."

A few seconds later, I have the biggest fire I have ever seen! I thank him, sit down near the heat and go on with my meal. He goes away, just to come back with a bottle of beer. I look at him, wondering what does he want. He says, "Hi, I am Anthony. Can I talk with you a while?" I do not have time to give an answer. He is leaning against the edge of my wooden table and begins to talk to me about his work here as a painter during the summer, about some incredible fishing stories, and about his fear of crowded big towns. He is surprised to learn that France is not under the equator!? After more than one hour I stop him and tell him that I need to retire. He leaves me, saying with a nice smile, "Maybe I will see you tomorrow."

I put my stuff in order and go get warm in my sleeping bag. I did not understand all the details of Anthony's stories, but I appreciated listening and trying to understand and talk. I want so much to learn English. Even if I did not feel at any time threatened by him, now that he is gone, I am more relaxed.

The cold temperature wakes me up early. I eat a quick breakfast and jump on Sam. Nothing better than exercise to get warm. Six miles later I am at Totem Bright. It is a state historical park, which contains fourteen restored or recarved totems and a colorful community house. The totems and the scenic coastline of the Tongass Narrows are beautiful. The sky is perfectly blue, the sea is royal blue, far away the mountains are blue also in the distance, and my nose is red in the cool of the marine wind. The totems are the eternal spectators of this gorgeous nature. Above them and me some bald eagles soar, finding the best ascending current to go always higher. I am again the only witness of this unique and awesome morning.

From here I come back to Ketchikan and find a sightseeing flight to Misty Fjord. I sit down at the back of a small, amphibious airplane with four other women and the pilot. Have you already experienced a takeoff from the water? Well, for all of you who do not know—it is bumpy. Every single little wavelet is like a rock and a shock for the plane and its passengers.

Finally we are in the air. I am relaxing a little bit. Oh boy, not for long. I feel my stomach goes up and all the rest of my body goes down. We hear the voice of the pilot in our headsets, "Bad news. We are going to have turbulence due to the wind. The good news is that this wind blew out all the clouds and we are going to have a gorgeous, perfect view of the scenery." We are shaken like cocktails, which makes me wonder which is the best: a perfect view of the scenery or a perfect flight? After a few more air pockets I have my answer. The thrilling beauty of the view makes me forget where I am and everything else. Now it is like floating in a dream. I see Ketchikan, this small "village" caught between earth and sea; it looks like the forest wants to push all the constructions into the water. Then we are above thousands of green small islands. Finally we admire Misty Fjord. It is a stunning spot with high, snow-covered mountains, falls, lakes; some of them are thawing. The high wind prevents the pilot to alight at the usual place, so he lands the plane on a peaceful lake (the landing was as smooth as the take off...). We slide slowly to the bank and stop. There is no room to walk, just big rocks building cliffs around the lake. We climb a few feet to stretch our legs and fill our lungs with pure air and peace. When it is time to come back in the plane, the lady seated at the front near the pilot gives me her seat. Was she being nice to me, or was she too scared to stay up front? I will never know, but I am so glad to see the take off maneuvers. It is much better for my stomach, but, also, for my eyes. What a fascinating view!

After another bumpy landing, I am back on terra firma in Ketchikan. I find Sam again, waiting patiently in the office of Taquan Air. The lady working here was kind enough to agree to keep one eye on him while I was gone. I bike back to my tent and light up a nice fire without Anthony's help! Well, for a French tourist it is not bad. I eat my pasta watching the intense newborn flames dying so fast. You do not need television when you have a fire... This night is very cold; my "super-anti-cold" sleeping bag is almost not enough. So, again, I get up early, and dress inside the sleeping bag—this requires some flexibility and contortion ability but with practice it can be done! Then I bike to Perseverance Lake. I do not have warm gloves (not very smart) and after fifteen minutes my hands are really numb. I try to hold the bike with one hand on the handlebars and the other in my pocket. This is not satisfactory, so I place my only wool jacket on the handlebar-bag and put my hands in the sleeves. It is working just fine. Again I leave Sam at the trail head.

The path to the lake is a narrow bridge a few inches above spongy ground. Again I will meet nobody during this hike. I walk in the dense silence of the rain forest. I can see some blue birds that have black heads and tufts. It is the first time I have seen this kind of bird, so I chase this rare winged creature with my camera for about twenty minutes. And finally I believe I have a good picture. I can say now that after this day I saw my "rare bird" everywhere. It is a Steller Blue Jay—a very common bird of the area!

I arrived at the view of the lake. It is magic. I sit on top of a pile of tree trunks, looking at the water. For an hour I admire the serenity of this place and view the real solid mountains right way up, and the reflection of the same perfect mountains, liquid and fragile the wrong way.

IV

Inside Passage

After two days in Ketchikan, in the middle of the afternoon, I board the ferry Malaspina for ten hours to Petersburg. Seated comfortably forward, I am watching the scene outside the big windows all around me; it is like an Omnimax movie, but here it is real. The sun sets. I am floating on limpid, dark blue water, which hugs the snow-capped Wrangell Mountains. Soon everything becomes pink, then purple. I see some dolphins jumping out of the water which is now golden. In a last effort before disappearing, the sun paints the surrounding nature with warm and intense color. It is a show that I will never be tired of.

Between Ketchikan and Petersburg, we stop for two hours at Wrangell (population 2,600), which is a cluster of canneries, shipping docks, lumber mills and logging tugs. The Russians founded the town in 1834. Later they leased it to the British, and finally it became American with the purchase of Alaska.

With two other passengers, we run almost one mile to the beach to see some petroglyphs. The petroglyphs are some primitive rock carvings believed to be 8,000 years old. The instigator of the "expedition" knows the area, and asks us to look for some 8,000-year old drawings on rocks with our flashlights! The night is really dark, and at first I think that it is a joke—like "looking for a needle in a haystack"! To my great surprise, after ten minutes we find three petroglyphs. There are about twenty in the area, and most are under water during high tide. We rush back to the boat. It was really quick, but interesting.

At one o'clock in the morning, we arrive at Petersburg. The lady I saw the petroglyphs with proposes that I share the room she reserved in town. I accept this nice invitation, which allows me to avoid looking for a campground in the middle of the night. We rendezvous at her hotel about one mile from the ferry terminal. She takes a cab. I take Sam. The time it takes her to disembark the boat and wait for her taxi is enough for me to arrive at the hotel a few minutes before her. Unfortunately, the hotel does not allow me to share the price of the room with the lady and I do not have the budget to pay a night in a hotel. So here I am in the cold of the night without any place to sleep at 2:00 a.m. Hoping I can sleep inside the waiting room, I decide to go back to the ferry terminal. I pedal as fast as I can to get warm. I see the light in the building. Wonderful. I sit down in a corner and begin to nap. At 3:00 a.m., an employee of the terminal tells me that he is closing the room and I need to go away. It will be open again at 7:00 a.m. Wondering what to do, I take my stuff and sit down outside on a bench on the porch of the building. I am completely alone. Since I do not know where to go and I am too tired to bike anywhere, I get into my sleeping bag on the bench and try to sleep. The cold prevents me from resting, and at 4:30 a.m. I get up to move and jump to get warm. I cannot stay here any longer; I take Sam for a ride. Searching where to go, I see an employee of the harbor. He tells me of a coffee shop in town that is open all night. If only I knew sooner! For the second time this night, I bike again from the ferry terminal to downtown. Boy! I appreciate the taste of warm coffee, a piece of lemon pie, and the heat of the place. All the customers are workers having breakfast before going to work. I cannot sleep here, but at least it is warm. The waitress allows me to leave my luggage here for the day.

With no sleep, but a light bicycle, I bike around the town first. Petersburg is called "Little Norway" because it was founded by Norwegians in 1897. The weathered boathouses, the houses built on pilings and Devil's Thumb peak among other snow-capped mountains give pretty scenery for pictures.

From here I go out of the town along the Wrangell Narrows. I stop at Blind River Rapids Recreation Area. I go for a short stroll along a boardwalk to the river. The boardwalk is above a bog (called muskeg). The area is one of the best fishing spots in the area where anglers catch trout, steelhead, and king and coho salmon. I am sorry to not have fishing gear! A few miles further there is a huge hatchery that raises thousands of salmon and sets them free. I go on further to Crystal Lake. Another pretty lake. Ocean, lake, river, falls...where there is water there is beauty. I savor a lonely lunch and then relax in the sun before getting back to Petersburg to take another ferry at midnight. I enjoy the rest of the evening writing, mailing post cards, and checking Sam. Today we did forty-two miles together.

I am on board half an hour before departure. First I take a good shower, and then I find a place to lay down. I do not hear anything during the departure, and sleep like a log until the break of day. In the morning, I meet Bill and Elaine from New Jersey. There are a wonderful couple in their sixties, and are very cheerful, youthful, and charming. Bill is diabetic and needs insulin several times per day. But they travel by themselves around Alaska. I love them. Neither age nor health problems prevent them from traveling. They are proof that nothing can stop brave, voluntary, passionate people. We spend the day together admiring the most beautiful part of the trip: the road to Sitka.

The sun is shining. For the first time, we leave the Inside Passage and turn around the Baranof Island to stop at the town of Sitka, which faces the Pacific Ocean. On the way, we pass close to Kruzof Island where I am very lucky (I am told) to have the chance to admire Mt. Edgecumbe completely exposed. Usually it is invisible under the clouds. It is an extinct volcano, which looks like Mt. Fuji, in Japan.

The ferry stops in Sitka for only three hours because it needs to wait for the tide. The Sergius Narrows, which we used to come to Sitka, is a tight waterway that ships must follow at slack tide. At any other time, it is too hazardous for vessels to negotiate the fierce currents caused by the changing of the tides.

From the ferry terminal, Bill, Elaine, the lady who wanted to share the room in Petersburg (I do not remember her name), and I take a taxi for a lightning-quick visit of Sitka. We admire the beautiful St. Michael's Cathedral. Built between 1844 and 1848, this church was for over one hundred years the finest Russian Orthodox cathedral in Alaska. In 1966 a fire destroyed it, but the people of Sitka saved all the treasures and rebuilt a replica of the original which we can see today. After the church, we walk to Castle Hill. It is here, on 18 October 1867, that the official transfer of Alaska from Russia to the U.S.A. took place.

It is now time to come back to the ship. We leave Sitka for Juneau. I enjoy this marvelous end of afternoon walking along the ferry decks, admiring again the Inside Passage. Suddenly, in a torrent of water, a whale jumps up like "Jack from the box"! My mouth is still open when a woman near me sees my surprised face and tells me this story. One day she was leaning on a boat rail, looking at the sea, when a whale jumped out of the water and plunged in again under her very nose, leaving her surprised, scared, and completely wet. She never forgot this trip! Whales, like dolphins, love jumping, turning in the air, and plunging again in a big splash. Their huge weight does not stop their playful mind.

It is 5:00 a.m. From the ferry landing I bike to the nearest campground and set my camp for two or three days. Then I bike to Juneau, thirteen miles further, as fast as I can because I hope to get here early enough to take a cruise to

Glacier Bay. Again the weather is beautiful, but the freshness of the early morning is here too. The road is pleasant, but after several problems of orientation, I arrive in town later than I had hoped.

Everything seems sleepy. I do not see the activity that one could expect from an important town. I ramble on the deserted boardwalk to this old shop where I can see some light. Inside, a smiling old man wishes me welcome. He seems as happy as I to find some company so early. He tells me about Davis Log Cabin, which is the tourism office. I follow his directions there, and find a small, wood cabin, a replica of the first Juneau public school, in the middle of the suburbs. A very kind lady inside enumerates all the wonderful things you can do from Juneau. I choose two one-day cruises, one for whales and the other for glaciers. I am disappointed that the Glacier Bay cruises did not begin yet, but I am certainly happy with my two reservations. Suddenly, I realize that maybe Bill and Elaine would be interested in these cruises, and it will be great to have their company too. I miss them. So, knowing the name of the place they are staying, I bike to the Alaskan Hotel. Elaine joins me in the lobby and appreciates my tourist's information. She doesn't know yet what they are going to do. I hope that I will see them again.

Now, let's go to Mendenhall Glacier—the famous Alaska drive-in glacier. I am biking happy like a bird, the sun shines, no traffic, the road is good. Everything is perfect.

Here is what I learn about the glacier: its length is twelve miles, its width is one and a half miles, and it towers more than one hundred feet above the surface of the Mendenhall Lake. Like an iceberg, the glacier is even more vast below the water. The lake is two hundred feet deep. The ice moves forward at an average rate of two feet per day, but at the same time, it regresses at a slightly faster rate, by melting and producing large pieces of ice, which float in the Mendenhall Lake. When the rate of melting exceeds the rate of advance, a glacier recedes. Mendenhall Glacier has been receding since the late 1700's, and retreats about twenty-five to thirty feet per year. It is incredible to realize that this gigantic avalanche, which appears to be frozen in time, is actually in perpetual change.

I take the West Side path, which goes up along the glacier, and soon I am above it. I can see the crevasses, icicles, sharp ridges, and pool of blue water. I climb always higher, looking for the observation point. I admire this fantastic view with my binoculars. It is like vertigo. I feel so minuscule in front of this giant of nature. It reminds me of the first time I observed the moon with a telescope: I looked through the lenses and saw the silver surface and the craters. It was fascinating! Then suddenly, as I thought about the distance between the moon and me, I felt like I was shrinking down to nothing—so much so that I had to close my eyes to recover. It was a strange experience.

O.K., let's go back on earth. So, here I am hypnotized by the grandeur of the scenery. After a few minutes I "wake up" and look for the path. I am in the middle of rocks. I cannot see where I came from. I cannot find the red ribbons that show the way. I try to look for familiar spots. Nothing. My heart is beating fast. Boy, I am lost. I am alone. I start to panic inside. Nothing hysterical—just a quiet, but intense fear arising from being completely lost. I close my eyes a few seconds and breathe deeply. Then slowly I go down a few rocks, looking feverishly around me, trying to see across the vegetation, searching for a clue. My eyes look everywhere at the same time when just there, I see it! Something red! A small, red ribbon attached to a branch of a bush, showing me the way. What a relief!

I am going down the trail thinking, "I came early in the season to not be bothered by bugs and crowds, well...it is working too well as far as people are concerned. Now I would like to see some humans while hiking!"

I gladly find Sam waiting for me, and ride back to my tent. Fifty miles, a good hike, and a nice dinner with the usual pasta give me a restful night—except a dream about being lost on the moon!

The next morning I come aboard a catamaran ready to watch for marine mammals and other wildlife. When I do not expect them anymore, Bill and Elaine arrive on board. I am so happy to have their company. First stop: Gustavus for some people who use the boat as a shuttle; then we go on for the others (the tourists).

Gustavus has a hundred and twenty residents who decided to give up on civilization and to live on their own in the middle of the woods. Electricity only arrived in the 1980s, and in most of the homes you still have to pump the water at the sink and build a fire before you can have a hot shower.

We go on to Point St. Adolphus, famous for whale observation. We wait for a long time without seeing anything. The guide of the excursion jokes about it, "the weather is too good for the marine mammals!" So, no whales, but I can admire the snow-capped mountains reflecting in turquoise water. Every day reveals more of nature's beauty.

On our way back, for the first time I see some sea otters. They watch us pass, floating on their backs with their cute little faces and their feet above the water. They are really adorable animals. They can dive three hundred feet looking for food, and then comfortably and carefree they dine on their belly like on a table. They are so cute.

The next day, again with Bill and Elaine, I take another small cruise boat (sixteen passengers) to Tracy Arm Fjord. This Fjord meanders for thirty miles, from saltwater to glacier ice. Today the weather is overcast, which adds a dramatic effect to this exceptional site. We progress in the narrow "arm". Close by on each side, a two thousand foot wall watches us pass with cold granite eyes. Then suddenly

I am touched to see them 'cry' pure waterfalls; touched also when I see them 'blush' some pink, tiny blooming flowerbeds. These gray rocks, green trees and bushes, white waterfalls, and pink, tiny flowers, are a fascinating mix of natural power and fragile beauty.

Moving deeper into the fjord, we begin to see some floating pieces of ice. As we go forward the pieces get bigger and bigger. I expect our boat to slow down, but not at all, we are going full speed straight into some big ice cubes. I feel and hear the sound of crashing ice against our hull. Then suddenly the engine stops and we glide quietly toward the South Sawyer Glacier. The melting ice allows us to go gently until we stop. I will never forget this one-hour and a half lunch stop.

In front of the boat I can see this huge ice mountain. I am hypnotized by its power. It seems that the ice flow and myself are stopped in time. I feel like if I move or even blink, the glacier is going to flow on us. I cannot stop staring at the scenery in front of me: a gigantic, unbelievable, shiny white sculpture of solidified water with a blue heart. One of the most striking features of a glacier is its blue color. Glacial ice has a crystalline structure that absorbs or reflects light. As light strikes the ice surface all colors of the spectrum are absorbed except blue, which is reflected back. I am bewitched by this blue, by the beauty of the moment. I am dreaming with my eyes open. Then it is my ears that start to dream. I hear rumble, roar, roll like a distant thunder. What is it? It is a big crash of a huge piece of ice, falling in the milky-green water of the fjord, just in front of us. I stay mouth open by the surprise. It is a forever memory.

My brain is satisfied; now it is time to satisfy my stomach. I grab a turkey sandwich (included in the cruise) and begin to look around the rest of the fjord. The giant ice cubes make perfect long-chairs for the seals. They lounge lazily on their white thrones. Some seals that are more brave, or maybe more curious, swim carefully toward our boat. They stop, however, at a reasonable distance and observe us. I wonder what they are thinking.

After this incredible live show of nature, we go on toward another arm of the fjord, which ends at the North Sawyer Glacier. The two glaciers are separated from each other by several miles. The North Glacier is not as impressive as his brother is. Am I already blasé?!

On our way back, we float between a bright, light gray sky, gray-green granite walls, green water, and shiny white or entirely blue icebergs. They are like some enormous, most precious stones, drifting until they melt. Again it is the beauty of the mix—power and fragility. These gigantic monsters of ice will slowly become soft pure, water.

On a rock not far away, the captain shows us a bald eagle. There are about twenty-five to thirty-five thousand in Alaska but less than six thousand in the rest of the U.S.A., where pesticides make them sterile. Now we admire some magnificent, colorful ducks. Then the captain puts our attention on a whale and its baby. Wow! It is another kind of wonderful show to see these huge animals swimming at water level, expiring powerful jets of 'steam' and diving for sometimes half an hour. The "standard" size humpback is fifty feet long and weighs around twenty-five to thirty tons. We follow "mummy and her big baby." They swim side by side, then disappear for a while. The noise of the expiration attracts our attention when they appear for an instant to slowly sink beneath the surface again, showing the symbol of wild nature and freedom—their famous tail.

We are back to Juneau in the evening, but this unforgettable day is not finished. On the boat today, I met Camille and Craig, a very nice young couple. They invite me to a salmon barbecue. My campground is thirteen miles away and I am concerned with biking late at night and I need to find a place to take a shower.

"No problem," they say. "Let's go have dinner right now and after, come with us to our home to take a shower. Then we will drive you back to the campground. How's that?"

"Thank you so much, but I am afraid to dirty your car with the bike."

"It's not a big deal, let's go eat," they say, smiling.

So here I am surrounded by the nicest people. The air smells of grilled salmon. The temperature is nice. Everybody is smiling. What a dream for a lonely canned-food eater! We choose our piece of fish and during the cooking time we walk around. There are birds of prey recovering from illness or accident, a closed gold mine, a creek where I play gold panning. No success... Well, I will get rich later!

We come back to eat our salmon; we choose a table and begin to enjoy. My God, it is so good. A woman comes to our table and asks to join us. Craig and Camille accept, smiling, and we visit all together. For American people, I guess it is not surprising or unusual. I will not speak for all the French of course, but for me, this unknown lady sitting at our table seems weird. I eat my salmon, smiling, and think if someone does that in France, people will be choked and wonder what does she want? American people are so open and friendly with new people at the first meeting.

So, during this unique time, I see people inviting themselves or being invited just to share a friendly social evening. What a lesson for a solitary French girl! Then adding to the warm feeling inside me, the sweet lady from the tourist office arrives and waves at me with a big smile. A stranger in this country, I spend a magic evening in the middle of friends that I did not know yesterday and that I will probably never see again...

In the cool of the evening, we leave to go to Camille and Craig's house. After my shower, I join them in their living room. My English at this time is so poor that it is frustrating. My French accent is also very pronounced, but we communicate eventually. The absence of vocabulary, in fact, gives me the chance to see in acts and on the expression of the faces, the kindness and hospitality of this couple. Sometimes, words complicate, hide, and maybe spoil the moment.

They drive me back to my "fabric-home." I try to express all my joy and gratefulness to them. Craig shakes my hand for a very long time, and Camille has tears in her eyes. I give her one of the little doilies that my grandmother made for me to thank people like them. I go to sleep this night (for the last time in Juneau) with a smile on my face.

The next day I am back on a ferry going towards Haines. Bill and Elaine are here also. We follow the longest and deepest fjord of the country, the Canal Lynn (seventy-five miles long). At 10:00 p.m., we arrive at Haines. It is very dark, no moon, and cold. I bike to the downtown campground five miles further. The first mile is difficult and scary because my bike's front light doesn't work and all the cars from the ferry pass very close to me one after another. The good side of this situation is that their lights help me to see the road. Then the last car passes and I am in absolute darkness. The next five miles seem so long. Finally, I see the city lights. Now I can see the road better. Oh! A female moose just crossed in front of me. She did not pay any attention to me. Boy! What a huge animal.

I bike through Haines without seeing any campground. It is so dark. After trying several ways, which lead me to dirt roads, I give up. I put my weather blanket on the dirt between a car and a big trailer carrying two jet skis, slide in my sleeping bag, and say, "Good night."

The freshness of the dawn wakes me up. I look around and now I can see a field of green grass. I bike there and realize that it is my campground. In the dark I couldn't see the sign, but the emptiness of the place also deceived me. I was looking for other tents, but nobody is here yet! It is 6:00 a.m. I unload the bike and leave everything near the little restroom house and go look around. The town (population 1,150) is surrounded by mountains: the jagged Cathedral Peaks of Chilkat Mountains, Chilkoot Range, and Mount Ripinsky. I learn that originally it was a stronghold of the wealthy Chilkat Tlingit Indians. The first white person to settle here was George Dickinson of the Northwest Trading Company in 1878. After him, missionaries and finally gold prospectors stampeded through the town. In 1897, Jack Dalton turned an old Indian trade route into a toll road for miners seeking an easier way to the Klondike (Canada). The traffic was heavy, and Jack Dalton reaped the profits until the White Pass & Yukon Railroad put him out of business in 1900.

After this educational moment, I spend the morning shopping and biking around until afternoon, when I join Bill and Elaine. They invite me to lunch, and we walk to Fort Seward. New educational moment: The army established Alaska's first permanent post at Haines in 1903 and for the next twenty years it was the only army post in Alaska. During World War II the fort was used as a rest camp, and in 1946 it was deactivated and declared surplus. In 1947, five World War II veterans and their families bought the eighty-five buildings and four hundred acres and gave a new life to the old fort. Finally, in 1970 it became part of the City of Haines, and two years later it was designated a national historic site.

Bill and Elaine go back to their hotel and I return to the campground. I dine and go to sleep early, this time inside my tent. I wake up at 6:00 a.m. As you can see, there are some habits that are hard to change. The good thing is that now I wake up every morning, not to go to work, but to discover the world.

It rained all through the night and it is still raining lightly. I unzip the door and look stupidly at my shoes, completely wet, because I forgot them outside... I pour the water out, try to absorb the rest with newspaper, and, finally, bike to the Laundromat with plastic bags as socks. Oh well!

Today Bill, Elaine, and I decide to fly to Skagway to go on an excursion with the White Pass & Yukon railway. We take a minuscule-little plane that really looks old and used. However, adventure is adventure and here we are in the air. The pilot flies his plane like a taxi driver. I mean he is so relaxed and confident that it is scary, because I would like him to pay more attention. At the same time, I guess it is reassuring, because if he is so relaxed it must be because there is no danger...

A little tense, but happy, we arrive at Skagway very quickly. Haines to Skagway by plane is nothing. Just the time to wonder if it was a good idea to take this plane and it is done!

Skagway (population 800) looks like the boomtown it was in the 1890's during the gold rush when there were over 40,000 gold-seekers headed to the Yukon by the Chilkoot trail or the White Pass trail.

I am sitting now on the train to White Pass Summit. The sunny weather changes as we climb from sea level to more than 2,800 feet. It gets colder and colder. The clouds are low, preventing me from appreciating the scenic road. There is also a lot of snow and the reflection of the daylight is intense. The most impressive thing during this trip is where the train crosses over some bridges. Through the window I can see the end of the train on this seemingly fragile construction above a very deep ravine. Brrr!! On some other bridges it is like we are suspended in the air. A really impressive railroad.

During the three-hour trip I learn that in the winter of 1897-98 some 3,000 pack animals were driven to death by over-anxious owners, and the White Pass was then called the "Dead Horse Trail." In 1887, the population was only two; ten years later, twenty thousand people lived in Skagway. An Irish contractor, Michael J. Heney, convinced some English investors that he could build a railroad over the White Pass to Whitehorse, Canada. From 1898 to 1900, the construction of the railroad was nothing short of a superhuman feat and became the focal point of the town's economy after the gold rush and during the military build up of World War II. In 1982 the line was shut down but revived in 1988 to the delight of the backpackers and the cruise-ship tourists. Skagway survives today on tourism.

Back in town, I follow Bill and Elaine to their hotel where I meet Sheila, another very kind lady who just drove on Haines Highway. I bombard her with a lot of questions about the state of the road, the place to camp, the hills, everything to try to prepare for my bicycle trip. She gives me her phone number in Vancouver and tells me to call if I need her and she will come and rescue me. It is so nice and so reassuring. I spend the evening with Bill and Elaine. It is our good-bye dinner. I knew that this day would come. I am so sad to leave them, but they have another road to follow, another destiny different from mine. I give a doily to Elaine. Bill wishes me good luck and stays at the hotel while Sheila and Elaine walk with me to the ferry. Good-bye, everyone! Tomorrow the real adventure begins. No more ferryboat. From now on, I need to pedal if I want to advance.

The ferry takes me back to Haines. It is late when I finally arrive at my tent but enough time to have a restful night.

V

What Bicycle-Touring Is About!

It is 8:00 a.m., Sam is loaded, and I am ready. The weather is sunny. I bike on Haines Highway to Haines Junction, which is one hundred fifty eight miles further. I can admire and never be bored by the surrounding mountains. Some ducks and bald eagles fly above me. Around noon, I stop at the only "grocery-like-store" until the British Columbian border. I eat and go back on the road. At 1:30 p.m., I arrive at the border. I see just a white, little house. I stop and go ask the only person here how the road is beyond and if there is a place where I can rest for the night. He tells me that the territory belongs to me and I will find all the space I want. Indeed! I wanted some space, and boy I tell you, I found it!

I bike on in the middle of the most beautiful, vast, stunning mountain scenery I ever saw. I begin to climb. For seven miles I keep climbing and looking for a place to set my tent for the night. I pass a sign indicating, "Next services 115 miles." There is a place to camp on the border between British Columbia and the Yukon Territory, as Sheila told me, but it is too far. I biked forty-seven miles already, and I can see that the ascension is far from finished. After a few more miles I see the first flat spot just big enough for the tent. Maybe it is where they store salt during the winter for the ice on the road. Anyway, it is the only suitable spot until now, and who knows when I will find another one. The highway is surrounded by deep ditches full of snow or melting snow, and right behind is the endless forest. I am not inclined to camp in the wood here, and even if I wanted I cannot cross the ditches with my heavy bike. I decide to stay on this flat spot. It is still early, but I have had enough for today. I lay my tent on the ground, sit down on it, and enjoy for almost four hours, the glacier-clad summits of what I believe is the Mount McDonnell. It is a privilege and a luxury to have the time to stop, observe, and admire this ocean of trees with the white range behind—like a gigantic wave. This afternoon for the first time, I think that I meditate without knowing it. I realize that I have the youth, the health, the passion, the nature, the peace, and the freedom in me and around me. I am happy.

It is around 7:00 p.m. and the sun is still high. I wanted to wait until the night to set the tent, but it is getting colder and I want to sleep.

The next morning, after an uneventful night and a good breakfast, I go back on the saddle and go on the ascension. It is rainy for a while. Then, climbing higher, the rain becomes snow. Completely crazy, do you think? Yes, you are right. You must have some insane motivation to push a one hundred-pound bicycle uphill in the snow...all alone. The truth is that I am not cold, because of the effort to climb and because I want to be here. I am happy to be here.

The road is going down for a while. It is, of course, wonderful to just let go and do a mile or two so fast, but the bad side is the cold. I sweat climbing and then going down brrr...the icy wind hits me like thousands of little needles.

I have to confess that I did not find the right way to dress, which could have sad consequences. When I was preparing my trip in the warmth and the comfort of my house, the correct clothing seemed unnecessary and too expensive

I was just complaining about the downhill? Well, I have no more complaints about that; the road goes up again...and up...and up...and *more* up...for hours, until I arrive to a sign that says: Chilkat Pass 3,393 feet. YESSSS!!!

At this point the sun appears and Haines Road flattens out, going only gently up and down. Soon I enter Kluane National Park. My goal is to reach Kathleen Lake, which supposedly has a campground with all facilities.

When I arrive there, I do not see any campground, only a large house and the lake. I take possession of a table and try to boil some water for my daily pasta. It is not easy with the wind from the lake. After a lot of patience I finally have my dinner ready. Slurping my spaghetti, I admire the snowbound Icefield Ranges of the Saint Elias Mountains surrounding the lake. After dinner, as I am writing about the eighty six miles of the day in my diary, a couple from the house comes by and tells me that it is a community building for visitors and I am welcome to sleep inside. I am so glad to learn this. I was ready to spend a very cold night. I bring my sleeping bag inside and we talk a little bit more. It is great to have some company. Since I left Haines two days ago, I spoke for two minutes with a couple of Germans at a viewpoint and saw four cars! I spend a good night, disturbed only momentarily by some other visitors who arrive in the middle of the night.

Early the next morning, while everybody is still asleep, I go quietly outside with Sam. I am eager to get to Haines Junction, which is just twenty-five miles away. For two hours I bike along the foot of the Kluane Ranges through a boreal forest of lodgepole pine and aspen. I stop at a big, wooden sign with a bear sculpted on it saying, "Welcome to Haines Junction." I am so pleased to finally be here. It is like finding water in the desert. I wanted to be alone. I wanted to have space, but after just two days I need to see a town, people, shops, a SHOWER...

From where I am standing by the sign I can see the town at the end of a wonderful descent with the formidable St. Elias Mountains on the left. I can see also the Alaska Highway vanishing far, far away. The sight, and the thought of being on this endless road soon, make me feel dizzy, but tomorrow is another day. Let's go! I jump on my bike and fly down to my oasis. I stop at the first motel, sliding on the gravel like a professional mountain-biker...well, almost...

The owner allows me to use a shower without taking a room. It is so great. Simple things are not appreciated until you miss them. So, you see, even the French can like to take a shower...sometimes!! Just kidding.

I go outside. A brand new Michelle takes a big breath, puts a big, satisfied smile on her face, and goes walking to the town's famous bakery. I leave Sam behind the motel. On my way, three backpacking girls ask me where to have breakfast. "Follow me," I say.

We sit outside on this sunny morning, enjoying muffins and pastries. Around us some cute birds, bright green with immaculate white bellies, are eating some crumbs. I love birds.

The girls are Canadian and are hitchhiking toward Whitehorse. We visit awhile, and they propose that I go for a hike with them this afternoon. I am pleased to have the opportunity to walk in company. The Auriol trailhead is eight miles from the town. We walk up the hill that I descended so fast with my bike a few hours earlier, and we begin our hike. The girls are twenty-five years old. They finished school and did not know what to do, so they decided to go to Whitehorse to find jobs for the summer. The trail becomes more and more snow covered, and at some point we have snow up to our knees. My feet are completely wet. Suddenly, Melissa, who is walking in front, stops and shows us a perfect bear print. I look at it and wonder if it is fresh, and where is the beast? Karen shows us a huge tear gas bomb that she has on her waist. She laughs with Melissa and they go on. The third girl, whose name is Ruth, and I get worried, but we follow, slowly, looking around and constantly expecting to meet the "monster." We reach a wonderful viewpoint. On the left, the Kluane Ranges stretch as far as my eyes can see. At their feet lies the Alaska Highway, and on the right there is what I will describe as a vast, flat plain. The amount of snow on the trail is increasing, so the two cowardly girls, Ruth and I, decide to go back to town. Melissa and Karen go on.

Ruth and I walk two hours together. We wonder if our friends are fine. It is getting late and they must be at least one hour behind us. Just as we arrive back in town, completely exhausted, a pick-up truck stops and here are our two girls jumping from the back, all smiling, and less tired than us! They hitchhiked back to Haines Junction.

Our shoes are completely wet. The "brave" girls have their trousers wet, too. They walked in the snow up to their waists and obviously did not meet the bear. We go to the Laundromat to dry our shoes. Forty minutes later, I give up. I put my shoes back on not quite dry. The reason for my impatience: I am hungry! When I am hungry I need to eat or I can be more dangerous than a bear!

The girls prefer to go in a bar, while I have some dinner. I promise to join them later—even if I do not like bars—because they have already set their tents in the woods and I am welcome to set mine with them. I do not have any idea where to sleep this night, so I accept the invitation.

When I meet up with the girls again later in the bar, we meet a man named Murray. He asks me what I am doing here. I explain my trip to him, so he tells me that he has a brother in Banff National Park, British Columbia, who is crazy about bicycles and that I could stop to see him and say, "Hello from Murray." We have a nice chat.

It is past my bedtime and I am getting tired; fortunately the girls are, too. So we walk (I push my bike) until the end of the town, then take a dirt road leading into the forest. The girls have trouble finding their tents. It is difficult for me to pass the bike through branches, dead trunks, and thick bushes. They wanted to hide: it is a success! Finally, we find their camp. I set mine, thank my friends for this great day and jump into my sleeping bag.

I cannot sleep. I feel very insecure here. The noises of the night are very close and frightening. After a few hours, I hear some growling, but I will never know what it was. Reality or imagination? The result is that I am awake most of the night, feeling the cold. I wait impatiently for the dawn so I can leave. As soon as I have enough visibility I gladly get on the road.

The Alaska Highway, from the viewpoint yesterday, looked wonderfully flat. Hum...like I was afraid, it is an optical illusion. The road climbs over several rolling summits. I need to motivate myself foot by foot. I am on my lowest gear and it is like the bike and my legs weigh tons. Every stroke is hard work, but the views are just outstanding.

After ten painful miles I reach a point where the road gets easier. On my left the mountains are so boundless that they seem close enough to touch. Since Haines I have been making noise to keep animals away. I sing (fortunately, nobody can hear me), ring the bicycle bell, or shout. It is working. I do not see any wild animals—not even a fly!

On my right now appears Kluane Lake, completely frozen. First, I thought it was a salt sea. It is such a bright white. After forty-seven miles I stop at the campground of the lake, hoping to find the same kind of community house as the one by Kathleen Lake. At the gate a big dog welcomes me. He has beautiful, thick, white fur. He shakes his tail, which is a good sign... He gives me a stick inviting me to play. I throw the toy many times until I arrive at the campground facilities. I see a woman wiping the front porch of a big building. I ask her if I can stay tonight. She says that it is closed. No water and no bathroom are available. I tell her that I am self-sufficient, and I just want a safe place to sleep. She allows me to set my tent. The dog has disappeared. The view of the frozen lake is gorgeous from here. Taking pictures with my telephoto lens, I see the dog near his master, in the middle of the lake. The man fishes in a hole he dug in the ice. I observe them a while, but with the cold wind beginning to blow, I retire.

Next morning the sun shines. I had a good night and my usual good breakfast. I bike alongside the frozen lake all morning. Some areas are melting, disclosing striking turquoise water. The sun is so intense that I have to put a scarf over my ears because they are already burnt. I pass Destruction Bay (population 46). I go on toward Burwash Landing (population 76). The only people I see here are two women working in the small museum that is almost ready to be opened. They are surprised to see their first visitor so soon in the season. The road is quite easy. I am surrounded by beauty. The world is perfect.

However, even in paradise everything has its end. After Kluane Wilderness Village I begin a new road of hell, which begins with the words: "ROAD CONSTRUCTION AHEAD." From now on I will not enjoy the scenery very much. I have to try to stay on the bike, to avoid the ruts, holes, rocks, and thick gravel. After seventy-three miles of rough treatment, I am forced to stop and wait for a pilot car, a vehicle that leads traffic. The road is in such bad shape that the pilot car carries me seven miles further near a campground (finally a little bit of luck today!).

I rush to the shower. I turn on the faucet and I stand still watching the warm and clean water turning brown before disappearing in the drain. For a few minutes I stay like this, looking at my feet, and letting the water refresh my body and my mind. I am really not tired, but I begin to experience some physical effects of the trip. My ears are burnt. I have a pain between my shoulders. My nose, the corners of my eyes, and my derriere are irritated! O.K., I just want to move you. It is the truth, but it is not so bad.

I wake up the next morning hoping that the good road is close by. I discover very quickly that, unfortunately, it is just the beginning. I put my scarf on my nose, sunglasses above it, cram my cap over all this, and go. More than ruts, rocks and gravel, the continuous washboard ground is the worst. It feels like I am on a jackhammer all the time. I am afraid my bike will fall into pieces at any time.

After a few hours on the bike, I see an old gas station with what looks like a general store. I go inside. An old couple lives here. The lady in her robe asks me to have breakfast with her. We talk about the wildness of the place. This couple lives in the middle of nowhere, completely isolated during the winter. However, instead of complaining, the lady describes the magical beauty of the trees, transformed each winter into crystal sculptures that the cold sun makes shine with all the colors of the rainbow...

I buy some fresh products like yogurt, pastry, and four eggs to go on my way. One hour later I have to stop and wait again to be carried a few miles further. They "throw" Sam in the back. Oh, boy, the eggs... The pilot car drops me where the road is supposedly acceptable. Yeah...maybe for automobiles, but not for bicycles! I wanted adventure: I got it. I decide to have lunch here, right where the pick-up drops me. The "woman-at-work" who takes care of the traffic is happy to join me and chat a while. When I leave she gives me her afternoon snack.

A few miles later, a blast of swirling wind and dust suddenly surrounds me. I have to stop and bend my head down in my shoulder. It is so violent that I cannot hold the bike upright, and Sam falls on his side. As quickly as it came, it is gone. It was like a "mini-tornado." To lift up Sam is extremely difficult. My heavy load is supposed to stay up! After many hard efforts I finally get Sam on his "rolling-feet." I thought that in Alaska I could become a snowman but not a dustman! I feel the dust even in my mouth. Fortunately as I was telling earlier, everything has an end—even hell! Like a dream, I now feel nice asphalt under my tires. It is so gooood!

I arrive at Beaver Creek around 5:00 p.m. The gas station is also an RV Park and accepts tents. After fifty miles on the dust I can take a shower, wash clothes and eat.

Some people who passed me on the road earlier and stopped here too, come and congratulate me for my courage to bike under the current road conditions. We visit a while and then I retire for a well-deserved rest. The next morning I am having breakfast when a man who spoke to me yesterday evening comes and proposes to transport me in his RV during the roadwork. It is so kind. I tell him that I will be fine; my only problem is that I woke up with a sore throat and a runny nose.

To my surprise, he runs back to his trailer. I begin to say, "It is not so bad, sir"... thinking that he doesn't want to catch my germs. I understand. But a few minutes later he is back with some pills to fight the cold, that his wife fixed me in a glass—ready to drink. How kind! I meet such wonderful people on the road.

After drinking my medicine, I begin a new day. The good asphalt ends after a few miles, and here I am again, trembling on the bike, bumping the ruts, eating dust. Deja vu!

Adding to my misfortune, a huge truck pulling a trailer of dirt goes back and forth between somewhere behind me and somewhere in front of me. So for more than three hours, this truck covers me with a new layer of dust each time it passes. Every fifteen minutes it is back, and gives me yet another coat of dirt! These back and forth trips must be distracting and funny for the driver, because after two trips he waves at me and blows his horn. "Sorry sir, I cannot smile, I have dirt on my teeth!"

My cold seems to get worse, my sinuses are irritated and I have difficulty swallowing. In this uncomfortable situation, I arrive at the Alaska border. I push Sam and try to find a suitable place to park him against a wall. A border agent comes toward me and yells, "Stop! Where are you going?"

"I just want to park my bicycle."

"Answer my question, I do not allow you to park the bike."

I am in a bad mood with the state of the road, the sinus infection, and I cannot express myself correctly. I want to show my passport, but the bike encumbers me. I do not move, showing that I am helpless. I believe he doesn't realize the weight of my "vehicle." After some thinking he tells me, "O.K. Leave the bike here."

I position Sam safely against the wall—I cannot risk that he falls down again—and follow the agent into the office. His colleague looks at my passport, smiles, and just says, "Thank you." Do they call this playing "good guy, bad guy"? Anyway, I go out shaking my head. I take Sam and we go on the non-paved Alaska Highway.

The two campgrounds indicated to me by some people at Beaver Creek are closed so I go on until Norway Junction. Here I find a campground and a grocery shop where I buy sinus nasal drops and pills. I am so sick that I set up my tent and go directly to sleep at 4:00 p.m. Seventy miles today.

I spend a very cold and agitated night. At 6:00 a.m., I pack everything and go to the "gas station-laundromat-grocery." I ask a native woman working here if she knows someone who is going to Tok, the next town that I think is a "real" town. I tell her that I have a fever and I need a doctor. She says that she will ask when people get gas. So, I wait, wait, and wait in the Laundromat. I can see that the few cars stopping here are not suitable to take my bike, or go the other way, or do not want to transport me, which I understand perfectly. At 11:00 a.m., I take the decision to bike to Tok. I see that the chance to find a ride with my bike is really low and I certainly do not want to spend another night here. It is too cold for a sick person. I cannot wait too much longer if I want to reach Tok before dark. I cover myself as much as I can and begin my "calvary." My head is just a ball of pain: head, throat, ears, nose—everything hurts. The sun is high. I am so hot. Every time I hear a car I show my thumb, full of hope, but very few cars pass me and none stop.

Around two o'clock in the afternoon a big, black pickup truck stops. The driver, who looks like a young Charles Bronson, asks me where I am going. I explain to him my situation. He says that he is going with his wife to Anchorage to work and that they can take me to Tok. We put the bike in the back and I go sit in the car near his wife.

I am so happy to be in a "comfortable," warm place. I say "comfortable" in inverted commas, because we are shaking so much that my teeth chatter! He drives so fast on the rough road that I hurt my head many times against the window. The wife is very quiet; just the husband talks to me. They are native Alaskans. I am glad that they do not want to talk too much, because it is difficult for me to understand their accent with my illness and the noise of the car. However, I learn that the woman is a nurse at Norway Junction. I will never know why the lady at the gas station did not tell me that there was an Indian Medical Center where I slept last night. The "nurse-wife" does not help me more with my problem. I am not complaining, because they take me away from my nightmare and I am very grateful for that. I am just surprised. Maybe it is because I am a foreigner and from a different culture.

We arrive at Tok and what I see disappoints me; there is an empty street where the wind blows away tumbleweeds. I do not want to stay here, so I ask if I can go on with them until Anchorage and share the gas expenses. They accept. During the trip to Anchorage, I can see the road where I would have biked for days and days and I thank my good angel for sending me this car. The road is really bad for hundreds of miles. The safe places to sleep are rare. Sick as I am, I wonder what would have happened to me if I had stayed at Tok. I am so glad to have taken my chance. I am so glad to be carried to the only town around here where

I can find a doctor, a hospital, or even take a plane to go back home.

So, I ride about two hundred miles in a shaking, black pickup truck with a couple of native Alaskans, two hunting guns on a rack at the back window, an eagle's leg swinging from the mirror, and the driver singing the Blues to the loud music of his audio tape. Exotic, is it not?

We arrive at Anchorage around 8:00 p.m. I feel weak. The couple asks me if I want to share the expenses of a room. I am so tired that I do not think too much and accept. We stop at a place where the wife leaves us to play Bingo. I do not know what it is, but that's what I understand. The husband and I go on to find a motel. We take a room and then he goes to rejoin his wife while I go directly to bed. What a horrible night! My entire head is sore. In the middle of a delirious nightmare caused by fever, I hear my roommates coming back quite late. I cannot go back to sleep, but at the same time I feel so tired. After an hour or two fighting against the sickness, I get up to ask for medical help. It is 4:30 a.m. The girl at the reception desk tries to explain to me about a place where the poor go for medical treatment. I do not understand very well. I am exhausted. I am scared. I want my mummy. I go back to the room and pack my stuff quietly, to not wake up the couple. I have decided to go home.

Finding the airport is another nightmare. I go the wrong way and I have to do a complete loop around the airport. I pedal two hours for nothing. The effort, the fever, and the frustration take control. I cry.

With sweat on my forehead, I finally arrive at the departure terminal at 11:00 a.m.! I ask for the earliest plane to Bordeaux, France. The very nice woman who takes care of me tells me that the best she can do is a plane tonight at 11:00 p.m. Twelve hours... The only thing I can do now is to be patient and rest. I spend the afternoon and the evening writing, sleeping, and between two headaches watching the television without understanding anything. I feel so sad to leave Alaska. There are so many fantastic scenery that I will not see. I promise myself that I will be back one way or another to the "Final Frontier."

It is time to board. I begin my trip back: Anchorage-Minneapolis-Detroit-Paris-Bordeaux. After thirty-six long hours and ten takeoffs and landings with sinusitis, I am back in Bordeaux. As you can imagine, I arrive at home so tired, so sick, but mostly, so disappointed. My family doctor examines me and tells me how good a job I have done to get a complete head infection. "You have sinusitis, bronchitis, laryngitis, and otitis—all in a very advanced stage." The doctor leaves my bedroom and here I am, lying on my bed looking at the ceiling, the very ceiling where everything began just a few months ago. I cry.

VI

Let's Try South

For a several days I stay in bed like a vegetable. I organized my trip so carefully. I thought of the worst of the worst, but I did not take antibiotics with me. How stupid! All this passion, motivation, and energy invested for a six months adventure, reduced to just one small one. I do not feel bad to have given up, because I will never play with my health for anything, but I feel so disappointed about my strength. I thought I was tougher, stronger. I clench my fists; I need to analyze rationally the situation.

This first experience by myself in a foreign country is teaching me a lot. I learn that I need people more than I ever thought, and that the bicycle part is difficult sometimes, but on average I am able to do it easily. I overestimated my ability to not get sick. I thought that, doing what I always dreamed, be free, my intense enthusiasm, the wonderful courage to change the current of my life, would protect me from any kind of bad luck.

The more I think about it, the more I convince myself that there must have been a reason. Getting sick has maybe protected me against something more dangerous. I guess I will never know for sure, but it is with this state of mind that I begin to see my situation differently. I got a lesson. I have to learn from it and try again.

After a few weeks I feel great: no more aches, cough, or runny nose. I am full of enthusiasm, to the dismay of my family, who hoped for a while that I was back to "normal," back on track. No, No, No! I did not finish my initiation yet.

I have so much to learn about the world and myself. I know that I have to go on. I decided where and how, but I still do not know why.

I study another tour from Denver to Los Angeles. If north was too hard, maybe south will be better. I did not plan for a second airfare to the U.S.A. in my budget, so I do odd jobs for a while and get ready physically and mentally for a new experience. At the end of August 1996, I put my cyclotour outfit back on and install Sam in his box again for a new adventure.

From the airport I follow a nice, flat road in a suburb of Denver. I stop at a traffic light and I see a prairie dog coming from a hole in the sidewalk. I see many more of them along the route. I stop for lunch at a supermarket and when I am ready to leave, I experience my first flat tire. I biked miles and miles on the rough roads of the Yukon and Alaska without one single flat. I cannot believe that it is happening now, after just two hours on a perfect road. I need to unload the bike completely to fix the problem. It takes me half an hour to be on the road again. The weather is changing. Some gray clouds are coming. I arrive in rain and storm at Cherry Creek Lake campground. I covered twenty-eight miles, which is fine for a new beginning.

It is now early in the afternoon. Very quickly it is sunny and warm enough to go swim in the lake. Then after resting a while I fix the damaged tube, set my tent and prepare my dinner. The weather is changing again. The wind is stronger and stronger; the sky is now a threatening black. I eat in the tent, worried about a big storm. My campsite is not protected very well against bad weather. I slip into my sleeping bag and wait. I hear some sirens and a voice from the loudspeaker of a car. I understand that it is risky to stay out because of high winds. Not reassured, I try to sleep. The wind is extremely strong, but fortunately, the tent stays up.

The next morning I eat a good breakfast with the sun and the singing birds. I am ready for another great day. I load Sam, climb on the bike, and find out that my front tire is flat. I stay cool. I unload the bike, remove the wheel, OOPS...I forgot the brake cables... O.K. Now I "open" one side of the tire, empty the saddle-bag to find the inner tube that I fixed yesterday, remove the flat one, put in the new one, check that it is correctly in place, pump, put back the wheel, reload the bike, OOPS...I forgot to refasten the brake cables... And to think that I had planned to leave early!

My goal today is to reach Chatfield Campground. The road goes up and down among fields with beautiful horses. I arrive at my destination quicker than I thought. Early in the afternoon, in fact, my tent is set up and I can rest, fix the damaged inner tube, and bike unloaded around the lake. Thirty-eight miles today.

A beautiful new day begins. Above me several balloons also enjoy this clear and early morning. After two hours heading to Colorado Springs, I begin to go up. My legs are amazingly weak and powerless. It is very hard to push both the bike and myself uphill. There is lot of traffic too. After half an hour of effort, I am exhausted. I step off the bike and push, and push, and push. When this position becomes too difficult, I bike up for a while, but then soon after I am walking and pushing again. I bike and walk, bike and walk like this for three hours. When I think that I have paid enough for today, the road becomes worse: dirt! In my mind, I see the title of this new movie: "Alaska Highway Nightmare II." Only now I realize that my Alaskan highway nightmare was pleasant compared to this: at least there I stayed on the bike. Here I cannot even pedal; I have to push Sam up because he is sinking in the dirt. For one and a half hours I just push up, stop, put a foot behind the front tire to prevent my heavy bike from sliding backward, take a breath, push a few feet further, stop again, get angry, push too hard, slide...and get my third flat. Bad luck!

After more than eight hours I arrive at a good road and a campground. There are no facilities, but there is the South Platte River, where I wash away the dust and the pain with delight (with goose bumps also)...but with delight!

I ask the neighbor from the next campsite where I can find drinking water. He says that there is none here and gives me some of his. I thank him. I fix my dinner and the damaged inner tube, then fall asleep. It was a hard day and I covered only thirty-four miles.

The next morning, the sun shines, the birds are singing and I am on asphalt. What more can I ask for? The road follows the river among trees. I stop at a campground to use a table for lunch and two women walking here ask me where I come from. They understand immediately that I am French—A*ii vonderr aouw*?! One of them invites me to lunch with her family. Her husband speaks French, because he has been a missionary in a French colony in Africa. They share their food with me and I share my adventure with them. It is one of the many reasons why I love touring on a bicycle. The hard times are quickly forgotten when I meet such nice people.

After this good company I head to Woodland Park. I arrive at a campground a few minutes before the rain. Like in many mountain areas, it is often rainy and stormy at the end of the afternoon in Colorado. It does not last long but it is here nearly every day. So after a short shower outside while I take mine inside, I set the tent and then go shopping. I traveled twenty miles today, very easily.

Waooo!! It is the next morning and I am flying. Fourteen miles downhill to Mannitou Springs. It is almost too fast. Never satisfied this French girl! At 9:30 a.m. I am at the Cog Railway where a train takes tourists to the summit of Pikes Peak (14,110 feet). I have two other options to go up there: hiking or biking. As you maybe guessed, I am not a mountain biker, and as you know also, my memories about dirt roads are not pleasant! I could hike, but the thought of going all alone puts me off. So as a lazy, cowardly girl I take the train. The weather is overcast and when we arrive at the top, it is snowing. In spite of this, I can see three beautiful, emerald lakes down below and a dozen cute marmots. On the way back I sit in front of a very nice couple from Tennessee. We talk all the way down.

After the unexpected snow, I bike in a perfect, warm, sunny afternoon to the Garden of the Gods. It is a scenic park at the base of Pike's Peak where the Great Plains meet the Rockies. I set my tent and go lightweight touring the area. At the trading post I see a beautiful porcelain Indian doll. My mother loves this kind of doll so I decide to send it to her as a surprise.

From there I go to Mannitou Springs. I like this town with all the iron, soda springs, pretty houses, flowers everywhere, and nice people. I spend the evening strolling around and retire after my easiest day on the bike, thirty miles without any effort.

The next morning I wake up very early to go take pictures of the sunrise in the Garden of the Gods. The weather is perfect. I can see the green valley of Mannitou Springs, with Pike's Peak behind, and the towering red sandstone of the Garden of the Gods in front. It is gorgeous. What I like in the United States are the contrasts of the scenery. You can see snow covered mountains with red hot desert at the base, or black fields of lava on one side and a green valley on the other side. It is always a surprise.

I enjoy the park all morning, then load Sam and before lunch I head to Seven Falls. I pass through old Colorado Springs. The last steep hill is a tough and long one. I was forced to climb a lot until here, but it is worth it. I can see all of Colorado Springs very well from above. Now I follow a nice shady road to the spectacular fall, which cascades down a steep canyon in seven distinct falls. I climb a one hundred eighty-five step stairway to the top, where the view is impressive. It is cool and peaceful in spite of some crowd.

I am ready to leave this beautiful spot when the lady from Tennessee, whom I met yesterday on the Pike's Peak train, waves at me. I am as surprised and happy as she to meet again. We exchange addresses.

It is time now to get on the road to find a campground. I bike all afternoon under a blazing sun, climbing one hill after another. I push and walk often because my left leg remembers painfully the last steep hill of Seven Falls. In the evening I find a place to pass the night after thirty miles.

The next morning I wake up Sam and leave the campground at 7:00 a.m. The road is magnificent with boundless, green prairies, the Sangre de Cristo Mountains behind and what looks like some wild sunflowers along the road. The temperature now is just right. My leg is completely recovered. "Vive la vie!"

My bike is so loaded that I go rather slowly. At this pace, I can appreciate fully the scenery, the fauna and the flora around me. I am looking down at the ground when I catch a glimpse of a big, black bug. I stop and go back to see what it is. Oh! It is a tarantula. She seems dead but not damaged. Maybe she is faking. I do not need to know if she is alive or not. I just take some very close pictures and go on my way.

I arrive at Canon City, perfect for lunch. At the grocery I ask some people about the condition of the road to Royal Gorge. There I meet a nice, old man who suggests that I stay at his daughter's place tonight. "Call her if you decide to spend the night at her place," he says, giving me her phone number. I thank him gratefully. After lunch I study the map and see that to find her place I need to go back. It is too early to stop. It is a hot but beautiful day, and I am eager to see the Royal Gorge. I decide to continue further.

There are more steep hills now and I bike very slowly. In the middle of the afternoon, I leave Sam for a three-mile ride to the edge of the gorge aboard the Royal Gorge

Scenic Railway. It is an open wagon train where you have the best view of the Arkansas River gorge and of the famous bridge. It is really impressive. The bridge seems so fragile from here. I can see the cars crossing and they look like little toys. It is a magnificent human realization. I come back to Sam and we go set our camp for the night after fifty miles.

The next morning around 7:00 a.m. as usual, we get back on the road. The weather is absolutely wonderful. After one hour I arrive at the closed gate of the bridge. It will open in a few minutes. The bridge was built in 1929 and because it is narrow, motor homes, vans, and cars with trailers are not permitted to cross it. I enjoy this beautiful, sunny, early morning, and when they open the gate, I take the boardwalk, pushing Sam beside me. A little tense, I walk slowly, glancing down. Below, I see only rocks. Then the rocks, little by little, get further and smaller until finally I am above...nothing for 1,053 feet and...plop! the Arkansas River. It is so awesome that I forget my tendency for vertigo and enjoy looking down at the river, which for this height looks like just a stream.

Fascinated by the scenery, I realize suddenly that someone is talking to me. I face the voice and see two young men from Texas, who want to weigh Sam. The first man reaches with one hand for the luggage rack buried under a mountain of stuff and tries to lift up Sam's "derriere." The bike does not move at all. He tries again with two hands and raises the wheel three inches from the ground. He laughs and asks his friend to try. They are amazed that I can bike with a load like this. I answer very cool that "it is a question of habit." In fact I am amazed myself! They ask me if they can take a picture, because I am an inspiration. I feel very proud and very good. I maybe give them the courage to realize some dreams, and they give me more enthusiasm and strength to go on mine. Good transaction.

I reach the other side of the bridge with a smile on my face. I step over my bike and decide to take a short cut. The road goes nicely down. I do not have to pedal, just look around, and enjoy a marvelous countryside with a nice breeze on my face. Bicycling can be heaven. I reach the main road toward Westcliffe. The nice breeze becomes scorching sun. I am pedaling in a live poster. Foreground: again the pretty, yellow, wild sunflowers. Middle ground: the beautiful Arkansas River. Background: prairies, green like a golf course, and even darker green hills. Then far away the Sangre de Cristo Mountains appear blue. All this beauty, lit up by the sun at its zenith.

After lunch I go on across this beautiful state of Colorado. During these long times alone on the bike, I think a lot. When the road is easy, I try to figure out what is really important to me. I try to decide what I want, to find ideas to make my life better. I think also about my family and friends. But when I am pushing this heavy bike against the gravity force or the wind, my only thoughts are about motivating my will, challenging my intellect, and then my stubbornness finishes the job.

I drink my last drop of water. It is very hot and I lose a lot of perspiration. Every mile I hope to see civilization. Two hours later, I arrive at Westcliffe with a very dry throat. I rush to the first supermarket and gulp down one liter of water so fast. I recover my breath and mind. The shop next to the market is the Chuck Wagon Trading Post. I love this kind of store. I go in and see the most beautiful Indian dolls, like my mother loves. The owner of the place, Roxanne, tells me that she created these dolls. It is a funny coincidence: as I said earlier, I sent one of this artist's dolls to my mother a few days ago from the Garden of the Gods and today I meet the artist herself; it is just amazing.

I ask Roxanne about a campground. The closest one is far away. I have already done fifty-five miles and I would love to stop soon, but if I have to go further to sleep safe and secure, of course, I will do it. She is so nice that she thinks of a RV Park closer and she tries to call to see if they accept tents. Unfortunately, she cannot get someone to answer the phone. Her employee and customers try to think about other suitable places. Everybody really struggles to help me and all speak at the same time. What nice people! Suddenly it is silent...and Roxanne says to me that she will drive me near a lake where she thinks I will be safe for the night. After some shopping, we unload the bike to put it in the back of her truck, because it is too heavy for us to lift fully loaded. I ride with Roxanne and her two children. On the way to the lake she asks me if I want to spend the night with her family. I accept.

At home she has a young girlfriend from South Africa who studies French. She baby-sits four other children, in addition to Roxanne's son and daughter! We take a dirt road for quite a while, going deeper and deeper into the boondocks. Finally, I see a beautiful, big, wooden house surrounded by the wild nature. What a place!

The weather changed, and it is rainy. We go inside. It is really nice and comfortable. I meet the baby-sitter, Mikie, and the other kids. I am so lucky to be in a cozy shelter for my first rainy night so far. Roxanne's husband is an airline pilot. It is why he is not here this week. She is a pretty and happy wife. It warms my heart to meet people like her. We spend the evening, me trying to get some translation of English vocabulary and Mikie learning French words. Again, at this time my English is so poor that we cannot have a philosophical conversation, but it is fun to be among kind, educated, happy people. Later, Roxanne's daughter lends me her pretty bedroom. I do not know why, but instead of having the best night of sleep in a real bed, I have the worst. Maybe it is the excitement of meeting these nice people, or maybe I cannot handle comfort anymore! I do not know. Anyway, it doesn't matter. I am so glad to know this family.

The next morning I see one of the most beautiful auroras of my life. From the huge, wooden balcony I admire the sun rising on the Sangre de Cristo Range. It is an enchantment of colors. From light pink to purple with yellow and orange. It is magic. I will not forget this moment.

Roxanne drives me back to town with Mikie. We hug good-bye and I get on the road. The weather is overcast, which is perfect for resting my sunburn and to keep the water cool longer. After sixty miles, a fourth flat tire, and with a sensitive bottom, I arrive at Walsensburg and set my tent in a RV Park. Suddenly the wind gets stronger and a big storm falls on the area. I dive into the tent, close all the zippers, and try to hold in place the pegs because the wind wants to lay them down. The rain is pouring and I am afraid that the water will finally penetrate inside. After half an hour of fighting with the elements, I give up and run to take refuge in the restroom. And it is just now that the weather decides to calm down! I come back to the tent and, of course, the side where the wind blew in is completely wet. But I was careful to put my stuff in the middle and, fortunately, everything stayed dry. The rest of the night is quiet.

Today I pedal toward Trinidad. The traffic is dense, but the road is flat. Forty miles later I arrive in town and stop at the tourist information office. They tell me about Raton Pass (7,834 feet) and then about the hot desert roads of New Mexico. It seems that the next weeks are going to be difficult, but I do not mind. I choose to be here and I enjoy it.

I find a campground in Trinidad. Before installing my tent, I go at the Laundromat. I spend the first part of the afternoon there. I write letters and in my journal. A man, also waiting for his clothes, speaks to me about a French couple who owns a ranch on the way to Raton. He even tries to call them to ask if I can visit them. Nobody answers the phone so he gives me their address for tomorrow. Here is another very nice person.

After the laundry, I go ask for a campsite for my tent. When I walk out of the campground office, six or seven men let me pass smiling. They look like workers. I hear the owner of the campground say to them, laughing, "Don't mess with her…" I am trying to understand. I do not know the word "mess." In French "messe" means "mass"!!! I do not get it!

I install my tent, eat inside, and go to sleep early, because of the mosquitoes and my "worker neighbors." I wake up at 3:15 a.m. because I need to go potty. Brr…it is cold outside. I put my blanket on my shoulders and walk to the restroom. Nobody around. On my way back I see a human shape sit down on the table near my tent. I grip my blanket tighter by reflex and act as if I do not see him. I pass as far as possible from the table, but the voice of the shape asks me,

"Can you give me a blanket?"

"Sorry I have just one," I answer, looking straight in front of me.

"I am very cold. Can you give me a blanket?"

I am near my tent. I jump inside, saying again, "Very sorry, just one." I close all the zippers. Inside, I stay still and wait, listening to figure out what he is doing.

I hear his step stopping near my tent, and he says, "I'll give you twenty dollars for your blanket."

"I have *one* blanket," I answer firmly, "If you are too cold, go in the bathroom. It is warm there."

"I don't want to go in the bathroom. I want to sleep with you."

I am scared, but also getting cranky, "No blanket for you. You cannot come in my tent, leave me alone."

"I am so cold," he insists.

I am really bothered now, "Enough now. I am tired. I have a long road tomorrow. Good night."

He stays here repeating the same story, asking the same questions. I do not answer or move anymore, and after a few long minutes he goes away. I breathe deeply, thank my guardian angel, and finish my night quietly with one eye open.

I do not have a lot of comments about this incident. Just that it is one of the risks of this trip and I am glad that it stayed just an incident. In fact, now I feel proud of myself for not panicking. Maybe not answering at all would have ended the problem sooner. I do not know. I am just grateful.

At 7:00 a.m., as you can guess, I open my tent with caution, hoping that all dangers are gone. Situation clear. Everybody is gone. I jump on Sam, after you know what: a good breakfast!

I bike to the French Ranch and try to find someone. I see nobody, so I go on and begin to climb slowly, but surely. The steepness and the front wind make the ascension not easy, but I feel good. I am almost at the summit of Raton Pass when a pickup truck stops in front of me and the driver offers me a ride across New Mexico to Alamogordo. He tells me that he has been on the road since early this morning and that he would appreciate some company.

I am here to bike and take my time, but I do not refuse immediately and think a while. The roads south across New Mexico are rather unfriendly to a slow and loaded bike. I am concerned about the heat, the absence of safe places to sleep between towns, getting water and ice, the coyotes, and the rattlesnakes. On the other hand, I do not know this man, and he may be more trouble than all the inconveniences of the desert...

After a few minutes of consideration, I convince myself that my guardian angel sent me help, like in Alaska, so I accept the ride. It seems crazy, I know, to accept a ride with a stranger any time. But even more after the scary experience last night. I have no excuse—just maybe an explanation: sometimes in life we do crazy things, because at that very moment they appear right or convenient. My trip by itself is crazy, so let us say that I am trusting my traveling intuition.

The truck is large so I sit against the passenger door, which gives me a lot of space between the driver and me. I hold on my lap my lethal weapon: a *heavy* Minolta 5000—very *heavy*—loaded with my "magnum" wide angle lens. I do not have to explain the damage to a nose, eye, or jaw if an aggressive face gets in contact with this kind of special material!

We head to Las Vegas, New Mexico. Mile after mile, like in Alaska, in fact, I do not regret one second to have chosen the easy way. The heat and the emptiness between towns are scary. We talk about the United States, France, economy, politics, and history. We cannot have a very elaborate conversation, but we have the time to try to understand each other. It is good exercise for me to be forced to express myself in English.

We arrive in Las Vegas at noon and I am invited to a nice restaurant. I am reluctant to accept, but he said that he is proud to have me as a guest. I am afraid to be impolite by refusing.

He likes the "Wild West American History" and he tells me that Las Vegas was a mercantile center on the Santa Fe Trail. During the 1880's, it was known as one of the roughest towns on the frontier with such desperados as Billy the Kid and Doc Holliday frequenting the area. With the arrival of the Santa Fe Railroad in 1879, the town became a major retail center.

After lunch we walk around the Old Town Plaza. The buildings are in the Victorian-period style, which you do not expect in this kind of old western town. I am so glad that this man wants to show me the interesting points of the trip. He tells me that he is so happy to have someone to talk with during this long trip from Denver to Alamogordo, which he does often and which is very boring alone. We go through Santa Rosa, Vaugh, Carrizozo, and finally, Alamogordo. There, I ask him to let me off at the KOA campground. He says that he was hoping that I would come to his mother's house a few miles further... This time I refuse as politely as I can. I do not want to push my luck too far.

I set my tent, very happy to be here. From Alamogordo I am going to take Highway 10 West, where it seems doable to find a place to sleep every night.

The next morning I hesitate to leave for Las Cruces immediately. Because of the unexpected ride through New Mexico, I am now further ahead on my route than I had planned. I decide to stay one day to visit Alamogordo, so in the morning I walk downtown. It is further than I thought and it is incredibly hot. After some shopping, on my way back to the campground, a lady stops her car near me and asks me if I want a ride. "It is too warm to stay outside," she says.

"I am not far now, thank you," I answer, always surprised and pleased to see the kindness of some people.

Back at "home" I take Sam, unloaded, and we climb a steep hill to reach the International Space Hall of Fame, which honors pioneers from many nations. It has a wonderful Omnimax theater and a shuttle camp. Outside it has launch vehicles and spacecraft. Also from here there is a great view of Alamogordo. On the right hand side far behind the town, I can see what looks like a bright, white line on the horizon. It is White Sands National Monument. After a few hours of enjoying the Space Center, I return to my tent, dine, and spend a nice, warm night.

At 5:30 a.m. I am already on the saddle. I want to make the most possible miles before the heatwave. It is dark. In the rearview mirror, I see the sun slowly rising above the Sacramento Mountains. It is fabulous! I stop many times to admire the scenery and take pictures. Now in the daylight, I can see that the road in front of me is flat and long, so long that it disappears on the horizon. I arrive at White Sands after fourteen miles without any effort. I come in the National Park ready to enjoy it.

Two miles later I have my fifth flat tire. I do not have time to get off the bike before I am assaulted by dive-bombing "Royal Air Mosquitoes." They are all over. I have to unload, remove the wheel, change the tire, put back the wheel, reload and at the same time fight these flying "pains in the derriere." It is getting warmer and warmer because of the temperature of the area and my impatience with the stinging enemy. I frantically try to find my bottle of repellent. Hallelujah! Here it is! I spray myself generously. It is working for a while. I fix the bike in record time and decide to get out of here. It is not the season for cycling. The man at the tollgate sees me pass by as if the devil was on my wheels!

VII

Timing Is Everything

I have been on the bike for three hours. The road in front of me is like a burning pool—a melting mirage. Far away, but getting closer, are the San Andres Mountains. I desperately look for some shade to stop for lunch. A few miles later, I give up and eat under the broiling sun. The biggest problem, however, is not the heat but again the bugging bugs. I eat in record time and quickly go back on the saddle again. No time to relax. In motion, actually, everything is better: it is cooler and the flying insects cannot catch me.

After thirty-three miles, I begin to climb the San Agustin Pass (5,719 feet). Every stroke is a victory. With obstinacy and sweat I reach the top. Hurrah! And then, "after effort, comfort," as we say in France. I am now flying down toward Las Cruces, eleven miles of downhill! I even have difficulty controlling the bike, especially when huge trucks go by. I stop in town to shop, thinking that my night stop is here. I ask confidently where the closest campground is. Answer: eight miles further. Boy, I thought I was finished for the day... As someone will tell me later, "If you want to play, you have to pay." So, I jump on the saddle...I am a little bit pretentious here. Let me try again: I sit carefully on the saddle—yes, it is much better—and go back on the road again.

After five miles, I am really tired—and now the road begins to go up seriously. I push hard on the pedals to advance; then a head wind comes into the dance, blowing dust in my face. My hands on the handle bar are as tight as my jaw. I look down and wrench the cranks inch by inch. I am so concentrated on not stopping—because if I do I will not be able to get up enough speed to pedal again and I will have to push—that I pass the entry of the campground without knowing it! Not too far past, though.

Ah, what a relief! I am so happy to stop, take a shower, and relax. I biked seventy-eight miles today. The evening is cloudy, but warm. My campsite neighbor is David from Ohio. We chat about his vacation and my tour. He congratulates me and wishes me good luck for the rest of the trip.

The next morning, I wake up at 5:00 a.m. I hear the rain patter on the fabric so I decide to go back to sleep. Nobody is waiting for me, no boss, no family, no friend. Nothing needs to be done, no tasks, no obligation, I can just listen to the rain as long as I want. I smile in the penumbra looking at the "pyramidal ceiling" so close to me; I am free.

One hour later it is still raining, but I get up and have breakfast inside the tent. Soon the rain stops and I leave with an overcast sky and encouragement from David.

The road is flat, straight to infinity, and the temperature is pleasant. These conditions are right to go fast, well...as fast as I possibly can; Sam and I are not aerodynamic! The numerous, huge Indian-owned tourist gift shops along the way are perfect to go to the restroom, relax, and refill my water bottles. After a tough day like yesterday, it is good to have an easy one today.

In the middle of the afternoon, I am pedaling easily on the emergency line, lost in thought, when a van stops in front of me. A man gets out, comes up to me, and says, "Do you need a ride?"

I smile, thinking in my head, "Again?!," but I answer this time, "No, thank you very much, I enjoy biking. The road and the weather are perfect."

He smiles and asks, "Do you want some fruit juice or water?" It is so nice, that I accept some juice. The man rushes to his vehicle, comes back, fills up one of my bottles and says good-bye. I wave at him and smile alone about such generosity.

I do not know what most American people would think about all the kindness their fellow citizens showed toward me. Was it luck that I ran into so many kind people? What I am thinking is that we are so accustomed to expect bandits, crooks, and liars, that when we meet really nice people, it seems suspect. Of course, unfortunately, bad people exist. I am not saying that everyone is nice and beautiful, that everything is peace and love, little birds and pretty flowers! But from this extremely naïve viewpoint, we are going to the other: everybody is bad and ugly, everything is war and hate, pollution and guns. What I am try to say is that it seems that if we just let people have a chance to honestly give or gratefully receive, we would realize that human beings are kind. There are good people all around. Regrettably, the media bombards us with violence and spitefulness and more regrettably still, we seem to like it. Crimes, wars, gossip, and perverted sex sell more than kindness, peace, or love.

This "philosophic" monologue makes me conclude that some people are genuinely good, some are really bad, and if they have a chance, the rest of the people will show goodness, but also excitement about catastrophes happening to others. *"C'est la vie."* (Such is life).

Anyway, based on my own experience of biking across the U.S.A., I am glad and proud to say that American people are awesome. They make me feel good about humankind.

I stop at Deming. I covered fifty-six miles today. It is still overcast and warm. The campground offers a metal shelter for tents. I understand why when I wake up the next morning. I unzip the tent's door and rub my eyes in disbelief: I do not remember installing the tent near a lake yesterday! It rained all night and now there is a river between the restroom and me! I am so glad about the metal roof because all my stuff stayed dry.

I leave Deming around 8:00 a.m. with a sky so low and cloudy that it is dark. I expect a heavy rain at any time. On the other hand the temperature is very nice and the road is flat. An endless desert surrounds me. However, desert does not mean nothingness. Along the road I can see dozens of different flower species—some yellow, some orange, some red, some pink, and some purple. Also, there are a lot of beautiful and colorful butterflies, unfortunately dying on the road. I am so sorry to see that. I still do not know the reason.

In the afternoon, I have my sixth flat. It is never easy for me to fix it, but on the freeway it is even more difficult. I am careful with the traffic and try to be as fast as possible. I arrive at Lordsburg after sixty-five miles and no rain.

After a restful night I am ready to take the road the next morning at 7:00 a.m. Except for the traffic the freeway has been a good road, flat and nice until now. But today I meet what I call "the bumpy lines", which are the gaps between the concrete plaques of the road. With an annoying cadence I jump up every two strokes: one, two, and up! One, two, and up! The freeway is not made for bicycles so...one, two, and up!

Around 10:00 a.m. I stop in front of the sign that reads "Arizona welcomes you." While taking a picture I am thinking, at least I know someone in this state: Rick of Arizona. I remember when I met him in Alaska and he was surprised that I was touring by myself without knowing anybody there. So like an inside joke, I smile alone in front of the state flag sign. Here, I know someone...

It is very, very hot now. I have to put a bandage on the top of my left hand, because it burns. On each side of the road, as far as the eye can see, is the green grass of the high desert. On the right far away are the Peloncillo Mountains.

There are almost no more flowers now, but I see beautiful yucca plants and, still, a lot of dead butterflies on the road. I see some dead snakes too.

Early in the afternoon I arrive at Bowie. Fifty-eight miles; my bottom hurts. But it is so early that I hesitate to stop. The next town, Wilcox, is twenty miles further. After resting for a moment, I decide to go for it. I follow the road along the left side of the Dos Cabezas Mountains.

At Wilcox I find a nice campground where I meet a couple from California. We talk while waiting to admire a storm in the distance. The air is very hot and heavy but the show is miles away above the Dos Cabezas Mountains. It is the blackest sky I have ever seen during daylight. The sun is setting at the same time. It is like the night and the day are two giants fighting against each other. We hear growling, lightning, and crying rain. What an unbelievable storm! Ultimately, the night wins and the day falls down blowing a high wind to our direction. Is the storm moving toward us? My companions go back inside their motorhome and I take refuge in the...bathroom, as usual! But soon I realize the fight is over so I return to my tent and everything stays calm for the rest of the night.

I spend the morning in town and after lunch I bike toward Benson. The sun arrives now with the west wind, which opens up the sky. It is good for clearing the clouds away, but I have to bike against this wind all afternoon. Five hours and sixty-three miles to reach Benson. This time, there are no more butterflies along the road, but I see huge, dead grasshoppers. I wonder why so many insects are dying along the highway.

After dinner, before going into my tent, I admire again the marvelous, starry sky. Where I live in France, the city lights always prevent me from enjoying the stars. But, here, in the dark, dark night, what a show the stars put on! It makes me feel humble, but also proud to be here to contemplate it and to be a little, little piece of the universe.

I leave Benson at 5:30 a.m. to avoid the heat and to have enough time to enjoy Tombstone, my next destination. I gladly leave the freeway to take a quieter and rolling road. Halfway to Tombstone, a Harley-Davidson motorbike passes me. I just hear the particular engine noise and I see a long braid of blond hair floating in the wind and a hand waving at me.

I go happily on my way. I pass a campground where I decide to come back tonight. I begin to climb the steep hill to Tombstone. I arrive just in time for lunch.

As a "lonesome cowgirl," I slowly dismount my "horse," attach it to the hitching post and walk along the wooden facades to Big Nose Kate's Saloon. My right hand is on my "lethal" camera, loaded with thirty-six caliber film. I am ready to shoot at any opportunity. The only thing missing is the sound of spurs on the boardwalk. Hey! Wait a second. Yes, I can hear some spurs. I look in front of me and see another cowgirl facing me. It is the Harley Davidson biker who passed me earlier. She has the complete Harley outfit and the noise of her black boots tricked my imagination. She comes to me smiling, and says "I can't believe you are already here." I smile too, and say "I am slow, but steady." We have a nice chat. She invites me to stop at her place if I am around Palm Springs later on. We wish each other good luck and go our separate routes.

I go inside Big Nose Kate's Saloon, dedicated to Doc Holiday's impetuous, tough, fearless girlfriend, and order a juicy, charbroiled beef burger with French fries, which by the way are not French in France but Belgian! "Miam! Miam!" (meaning Mmmm! Mmmm!). My hunger satisfied, I can begin discovering the rest of the town.

Tombstone is like the American West I watched on TV, except that it is not fake. It is real. The original 1880's buildings are well preserved. When Ed Schieffelin came to Camp Huachuca with a party of soldiers and left the fort to prospect, his comrades told him that he would find his

TO CHILKAT PASS (3,393 FEET)

ALONE IN ALASKA

BLUE ICEBERG

INSIDE PASSAGE

SUN RISING ON THE SANGRE CRISTO RANGE

TWO BANDANAS AS SLEEVES

FIGHT BETWEEN DAY AND NIGHT

MAGIC DUSK

SAM IN ARIZONA

TO SAN AUGUSTIN PASS (5,719 FEET)

SUPERSTITION MOUNTAINS

SAGUARD NATIONAL PARK

THE MORNING BEFORE MEETING RALPH

ME AND RALPH

TO CALIFORNIA

tombstone rather than silver. In 1877, he named his first claim "Tombstone," and rumors of rich strikes made a boomtown of the settlement that adopted this name. For seven years the mines produced millions of dollars in silver and gold. Production suddenly came to an end because of rising underground waters.

On Allen Street, in front of the O.K. Corral, I see a sign indicating where Billy Clanton died on Oct. 26, 1881. Along the street I see signs showing where the other members of the gang fell. It is so funny to be in this American West ambiance. All the famous movies about it made me forget that lawlessness and violence really existed. But anyway, it is amusing to see the Birdcage Theater, built in 1881 and still unchanged; you can see the original fixtures, furnishings, and bullet marks in the wall! You can see also the original equipment and presses of the West's most famous newspaper, *The Tombstone Epitaph*. On Toughnut Street I see the world's largest rosebush which covers more than 8,600 square feet. The white-blossomed shrub was planted as a cutting sent from Scotland about 1885. You can see the big stalk going up and thousands of branches shooting out of it, making the biggest arbor you ever saw. It is really incredible.

In the evening, on my way to the campground, I stop at Boothill Graveyard. There are two hundred and fifty marked graves of early citizens, as well as graves of some of the town's famous and infamous residents. I must say that, although the cemetery tells the sad story of a lawless, violent time, some of the epitaphs make me laugh. I have to confess that for me, because of the Hollywood movies, it is really symbolic of the Wild West. Here are some of the surprising epitaphs: *Suicide; Shot by Sheriff Behan; Killed by Apaches; Drowned; Hanged; Hanged by mistake...*

From the cemetery, I fly downhill to the campground. I get in my sleeping-bag and immediately fell asleep. After dreaming that an unlucky Apache was hung by mistake, then drowned, then shot by the Sheriff, I wake up and ready to leave at 6:30 a.m. I need to buy some ice but I do not feel like climbing the steep hill to Tombstone again. I see the town of Fairbank on the map, eight miles from here. I will be there before the heat, so I decide to go ahead. The road across the Coronado National Forest is simply beautiful. I enjoy it a lot until the sun begins to warm up significantly, and I do not see any town yet. Mile after mile I get more and more concerned about finding some ice. My water is getting warmer and soon I will not have any. It is really strange. I feel like I did in Alaska, when there was nothing for hundreds miles around me. And as a joke, the town I am looking for is Fairbank (without s). Sometimes life is so ironic. Thirteen miles since Tombstone and I have seen nothing except the San Pedro River, two or three cars, and four tombs alongside the road.

I am very angry with myself for not returning to Tombstone this morning. I grumble, make faces, and mimic my thoughts from this morning out loud, "The hill is too steep. You will find some ice in the next town." I shake my head and berate myself, "You lazy girl! How stupid of you! It is a good lesson, dummy. You should never go without ice for more than sixty miles on an isolated road, and knowing that it is going to be extremely hot, for crying out loud!"

"But I thought I would find this Fairbank town sooner," I answer myself.

"Thinking is not enough, you have to always be prepared, and always have the basic needs with you. I hope you are going to suffer enough to remember."

Boy, I am tough with myself! I am glad that nobody sees me talking alone. They will think that I am completely mad.

After my self-punishment monologue and a few more miles, the anger becomes anxiety. Just when I am getting really worried, I see one house, then another. What a relief! I accelerate the cadence. There must be a store, a gas station nearby, or someone from whom I can buy ice and water. And here it is, my rescue town. I rush to the store as if my life depended on it and buy ice, water, and a cookie. I walk out of the store, looking outside and closing the door behind me, when I feel the door resisting. I look back over my shoulder and I cannot believe what I see. You will not believe it yourself, but it is the truth. I am not going to keep the suspense further, but just tell you what happened.

"Hey... Hello Rick!" I say.

He looks at me like I am a ghost, and stutters, "I...I can't believe it...I can't believe it." He goes on, talking to the surprised cashier, "I know this girl, I know her; she comes from Alaska...on a bicycle!"

"Not really," I answer smiling.

We go outside. Rick looks at me, looks at the bike and then looks at me again, saying "I just can't believe it."

"I stayed just one month in Alaska, got sick, went back to France and started again from Denver," I tell him.

"Denver? I can't believe it."

"And you? What happened? I thought you still were in Ketchikan. It is so strange. I thought of you when I saw the Arizona State sign. What a surprise!"

"It was not satisfactory working there so I came back here after a month also. Now I am working for a truck company... I just can't believe it. I came here to get some gasoline. I live close by in Huachuca City, but I never come here. Incredible..."

"I left Tombstone this morning without ice and I was getting worried to not find any place to buy some. This town is not on my map..."

We stay silent a second and then Rick says, "It is really incredible. Small world... Well, I need to go to work now. Let's exchange our addresses because I want to know more about your trip."

"Sure, I want to know also about your experience in Alaska."

"Bye," says Rick walking away.

"Bye," I answer, my heart beating hard.

He goes back to his car and goes on his way and I go back to my bike and go on my way. I have been so cool until now, but suddenly I am euphoric. I feel so light and happy that it feels like the bike, the load, and my body weigh nothing. I am pedaling fast with no effort, a big smile on my face. My thoughts go as fast as my feet. It is a magic moment. It is The Magic Moment of my life. How many chances to meet again? The window of opportunity is so small. One or two minutes before or after and we would have never known that we were so close to seeing each other. If I had been a responsible girl and climbed the hill to buy ice, I would have missed him. If he had bought fuel at his usual place, he would have missed me. I do not know by which mystery we made it. It was meant to be. In France we say: "Never two without three." It means that when something happens two times, it will happen a third time. So maybe we will meet somewhere again.

I pedal away from this incredible coincidence, suddenly wondering if what I am looking for—without knowing—is a mate! This idea confuses me a lot.

I am rather...strange or maybe just unusual. I am twenty-nine years old. And as I was telling you at the beginning, I have had a sheltered life. My family, some friends, and colleagues gave me all I needed. Frankly, I have been and still am a lucky and happy girl. It is the routine, some dissatisfaction, and my insane passion for travels that gave me the courage to try this adventure. When planning for this trip, I did not think about romance for one second. My life until now was family oriented. Most of my cousins, who are all around the same age as I, live two or three miles from my parents' house. My childhood girlfriend is my next door neighbor. So, I did not have to go to the "outside world" to play.

Of course, as you would expect, I *was* exposed to the "outside world" in school. The truth is, I was so hurt the day my grandmother left me with a bunch of small strangers, and I could no longer have the daily joy of staying with her. I was five, but I will not forget the pain of feeling betrayed and the fear of being in this unknown, new world. Since then, I never liked school. I expressed my childhood pain with stubbornness. I never wanted to understand the benefits of school. Many times my parents tried to explain to me that being a good student would help me have a good life. I never failed to do my homework, but it was because I was terrified to be reprimanded by my teachers, not because I believed it was beneficial for me. And I was told that if I did not go to school the "gendarmes" would come and get me. So, I went to school, learned, and behaved just enough to graduate, waiting for the bell to ring at the end of the school day. I made some friends of course, but my cousins were also in the same school and one was even in the same classroom so I still spent a lot of time with family.

All these details are to say that my social life was and is my family life, and I like it this way. I stayed a child longer than normal and I never had the need to flirt with boys. Then growing up, and understanding better, I became afraid of the truths of life. Until now, I protected myself by being what I call "invisible". In school, at my different jobs, and when I travel (especially on this adventure) I make every effort to hide, to not expose myself to any awkward situation. While most women try to look their prettiest when in company, I do nothing to improve my mediocre appearance. The fear of the unknown and the risks of intimacy put me way back in my shell with a proud sign outside: "I want someone to love me like I am, not with a pretty disguise." The problem with my attitude, I realize now, is that if by a miracle a man should look at me, he will not see me like I am. He will see a shell! Not very attractive is it?

I wanted to protect myself...well, it worked perfectly! Twenty-nine years old and no, none, nada, intimate relations with any man. Friendship or working relations with men are no problem, I am the best at that. I worked for ten years as a secretary in a big construction company with hundreds of men—engineers, architects, subcontractors, workers, colleagues, customers—and never any ambiguity; my dealings with all of them were always straightforward. I am invisible as a woman; I am just a "nice person".

I just said that I never had any intimate relationship with a man...in fact...I lied a little bit, or rather I did not say the entire truth, but how can you believe my story if I do not say the truth, the entire truth? What I was ready to omit from my story, was a short flirting experience.

One time, a friend, who maybe liked my "shell" decided to look closer and wanted to kiss me. I liked him a lot, but when I saw his lips one-inch from mine, I could not do it. I nervously laughed and told him that I could not do it. He was a gentleman and did not insist. We talked about it and ended an intimate story before it even began and went back to our friendship. I was too scared.

I come back now to my magic moment with Rick. I hope you understand better my confusion. The goal of my bike adventure is to do something different, to find ideas which will change my life or my vision of it, to find what will make me happy. However, I never thought about romance.

When I met Rick the first time I found him attractive. A good-looking young man, ready for adventures in Alaska. Like some story's hero. The magic of this second improbable meeting infatuates me. I am floating in the air on a flying carpet, laughing, crying, and making plans about a correspondence with "Rick of Arizona."

I am in a dream. I do not see the miles streaming by, and I do not feel the hills. I arrive at a dirt road surrounded by gorgeous scenery. I usually hate dirt roads but this one doesn't frighten me. I even smile, thinking that I am going to flatten a tire at every shock. Today is my magic day.

I am in the middle of beautiful mountains with cactus, yuccas and then, fields of flowers. I stop to push Sam carefully across a cattle crossing—these grills across the road are annoying for a bicycle—and I arrive at a sign saying: "Open Range." I do not understand what it means, until I see the cows and a magnificent longhorn on the road. His beauty and force are so fascinating that I almost forget to be afraid. I am so happy anyway that the fear doesn't control me and I pass in front of the beast as quietly as possible, almost confident.

After the magic moment of my life, biking up and down sixty miles on a mostly dirt road that I had to share with cattle, you know what? I am tired! However I cannot stop and rest yet. A sign indicates a campground four miles further, uphill. I spent the day biking without any effort and now, boy!, it is so hard. It is as if suddenly my bike doubled in weight. My nose is bent over the handlebars. I push and push on the pedals with my legs. I pull and pull on the handlebars with my arms. I cannot believe that it is so difficult. After two miles of fighting, exhausted, I step off the bike and see that my rear tire is completely flat. I was so much under the spell of this magic day that I did not notice the problem, and biked for miles on the rim...OOPS!

I push my load up for the next two miles and finally I arrive at a suitable place before the campground. I do not have the strength to go on. Completely worn-out, I decide to stop right here. Boy, what a day! I fall asleep very quickly after my dinner and my dreams are about one "Rick of Arizona."

I wake up early the next morning, eat breakfast, and fix my tire. When I think about all the horrible dirt my poor Sam took in the wheels, I wonder how I did not have more flat tires yesterday. After this quick concern about Sam, my thoughts quickly go back to Rick. I still do not believe it. But it is time to go back on the saddle.

Yesterday's weary climb to the campground is now a wonderful downhill to get back on the main road, which makes me invent a deep thought: "What one climbs today will be descent the next day." Proud of my silly proverb, I am carried away by the descent.

The road is full of bumps and ruts, and the bike and I are jolted. I am holding on tight and focusing on the road, when I see my camera bag about to fall from the handlebars. All my precious things are in this bag. What happens now takes half a second, but I experience it in slow motion. I see the bag ready to fall in front of me. I do not want to roll over it and risk a fall and at the same time damage all my important things. So I have the idea, or the reflex, to move the handle bar violently to the right, which projects the bag to the side of the road. OLE! I brake hard, slide, and finally stop.

Assuming the worst, I walk back to my bag and stare at the horrible scene. My precious camera has its "nose" in the mud. My walkman has its "belly" open, the broken cassette lying on one side, the two batteries on the other side, and my journal, maps, letters to send, and important papers are wet. My mug of water, which I attach every day to my handlebars with a scarf, has exploded and wet everything. What a disaster! After I recover from the shock and my heart beating back to normal pace, I thank my lucky star again. I did not get hurt, which is the most important thing. I put my Walkman back together, and find out with surprise that it is working. The papers will dry soon, but I am devastated about my camera. I clean the mud, dirt, and water off. I put everything back in place, check five times that the bag is correctly hooked, and get back on the bike. I hold the brakes to go as slowly as possible. I do not roll three quarters of a mile, when I feel my rear tire deflating. This time I feel it right away! The earlier scary incident put me back on earth. My flying carpet has landed. Hello! It is reality and it is time to wake up. So...I unload the bike and...I will spare you from the usual procedure; let's go on with the day.

After about thirteen miles, I arrive at a town named Continental, where I buy some ice and where my tire deflates again. I am too tired to unload, blab, blab, blab, and reload so I decide to correct the problem by just pumping. My "smart" decision leads me to stop and pump every half mile until I run out of patience and I stop again, unload, remove the inner tube, check the tire and find the reason of my morning in hell: an ugly staple. I do not know how I missed it when I checked the tire last time, but anyway, at least my problem is solved. It is almost with some enthusiasm that, once again, I go into the tire-fixing procedure. Ready now to finally go somewhere, I jump on the saddle and...ten feet further I am flat again.

Oh! Now I am really angry. I want to kick the bike and throw it away. Who wants to test my patience? Who plays this game with me? It is not funny and I am tired of it. After this understandably violent reaction, I calm down and, guess what? I re-unload the bike etc., etc...

Everything is on the ground again and I am so discouraged that I decide to eat. It is lunchtime anyway. My stomach satisfied helps me to return to normal behavior. And so, like a robot I fix the tire again. Then instead of reloading my stuff, I decide to try the bike first. "What a genius idea, Michelle!" says a sarcastic voice in my head. "Why did you not think about it before?" I mumble to myself, " No comment, please."

I pedal a little while and come back to where my stuff is spread out on the ground. Everything seems all right. I reload Sam, and I get on the bike very carefully. Crossing my fingers mentally I begin to roll. It will be my last flat. I think that earlier, with the irritation of the moment, I must have put back the pierced inner tube instead of the spare good one, and that is why I was flat after finding the staple in the tire...

Now and then, I begin to see some typical saguaro cactuses and suddenly far away two bright white towers. It is "the white dove of the desert," Mission San Xavier. The first view is breathtaking. It is so beautiful. The whiteness is extraordinary. It looks like a mirage. I can imagine pilgrims after a tiring day walking in the heat and dust, suddenly looking up and seeing the white house of God, where they are going to find rest, peace, and coolness. Like them, I come into the Mission San Xavier. The opulent style inside, with its predominant colors red and golden, busy columns, and numerous niches, contrasts with the simplicity of the exterior. Back outside, I wonder, as everybody does, why one of the bell towers is not finished. Some say that the Spanish Crown would have taxed the building when completed, and it was for this reason that the padres never finished it. Others say that they simply ran out of money.

After the mission, I go on toward Tucson and enter into the Saguaro National Park. It is very hot, the sky is intensely blue, the soil is red, and the hills around are covered by the giant saguaro cactuses (see pictures). It is like the hills are covered with giant needles and the needles are themselves covered by smaller needles. Some of the saguaro are so funny with their long noses and arched arms. They really look like some clowns who would like to take you in their arms, but I do not think it will be funny to be hugged by them! They have a likable posture, but an inhospitable texture. Some have small holes where birds make their nests. The saguaros can live two hundred years and attain 30 or 40 feet heights. Pedaling along in this amazing environment, I find a campground where I stop for the evening. I am surrounded by all kinds of different cactuses. It is superb, and the sunset adds its magic. Unique warm colors make the end of this day unforgettable.

After a peaceful night I go back on my "thorny" road. This early morning is perfect to enjoy the park. After a few hours, I leave the Saguaro Park, but not the typical flora. I arrive at Picacho Peak Park after lunch. I decide to rest in the nice campground and enjoy the swimming pool. It is too hot to do anything else. And fifty-four miles satisfies me.

The next day I hesitate between going on towards the West, and making a detour by Roosevelt Lake. My trip through New Mexico is going much faster than I had planned because of the ride in the pickup truck, so I decide to change my itinerary.

VIII

The Garage of Hell

The flat road allows me to pedal at a good rate. I am on my way to Roosevelt Lake. After a while I begin to cough a lot. The air is full of little white flakes. I do not know what it is. It seems to come from this huge field I am crossing. It is so annoying that I have to bike with a scarf on my face. Thirty miles further I arrive at Florence (elevation 1,493 feet), a very pretty, old town built in 1866. After Florence Junction, the crossroads about twenty miles from the town, the road starts to climb through the Tonto Forest. It is very, very hot. I drink a lot and soon I run out of ice. I am sweating liters of water. I am wondering when I am going to find ice when a fast cyclist passes me just like the Road Runner—beep! beep!—passes Wile E. Coyote. Then another, and another passes me. Am I in the middle of a race, or what? One of the racers slows down and chats with me. They all belong to a cycling club, touring from San Diego to Charleston! They bike about one hundred twenty-five miles per day. He tells me that a few miles further they have a food and water stop. I am too slow for him, so after this nice chat he leaves me quickly behind. His light road bike just flies up the hill so easily. I am very happy to know about a water stop and I thank my lucky star again. How could I dream that just when I run out of cold water on this endless hill, a bicycle caravan, complete with food and water, would appear?

Indeed, twenty-five minutes later, I see a van on the side of the road carrying spare wheels and bicycles. There are tables with fruits, energy bars, and water. I arrive there exhausted by the climb, but especially by the heat. I do not have the time to say anything when a woman comes to me and puts some sun-protection cream on my face and my hands. Another brings me water. I could never dream of receiving this kind of help. We visit a few minutes. Then I am ready to go on, and they need to move to the next stop. In fact, they were waiting for me. The racer who slowed down to talk with me back on the road told them I was coming. I will not surprise anybody if I say that I am the last biker!

As usual, after I stop facing uphill, I need to first go downhill to get on the bicycle and gather some speed, then make a U-turn to take back the ascent. I have nicknamed this ingenious maneuver "the Sicard Start"; it lacks in style and grace but it works. Sam is so heavy that I cannot get on him and begin pedaling while going up a steep hill. I tried and failed every time; the bike tips over and I stand, all embarrassed, with Sam between my legs. And when Sam is on his side, it takes two Hercules to put him back on his wheels. One to lift up the weight, and one to keep the load together.

After this marvelous, convenient help from the caravan, I am back climbing. I go as fast as I can to try to be on time at the next "service stop." It is hard, but it is encouraging to think that I am not making this ascension alone in this sultry weather.

After some difficult miles, I arrive at a town named Superior (elevation 2,730 feet). I stop to eat and find many racers already devouring some hamburgers. They are surprised to see me. I must look so funny with my round face all red, my clownish shorts, my long sleeve shirt with fringes, my Birkenstock shoes, my cap crammed down to my eyes, and my thighs red like a boiled lobster. The rest of my legs do not take the same amount of sun, so it looks like I have socks until the knees. To say the least, I do not have the cyclist style! After my snack I go back on the road. The climbing gets steeper and steeper. I push all out for miles, and finishing a sharp turn I see the cycling club's van still there, at the next "service stop". They congratulate me and invite me to their dinner tonight at Globe. I look on the map and see that it is too far for me to reach this town in time; I decline their kind invitation. They ask me if I need anything, and I answer "Yes, please!" They fill up my bottles with water, my mini-cooler with ice, and my brain with motivation.

I execute a perfect "Sicard Start" and return to the climb. A few minutes after my departure, I hear the horn of the van. They pass me, waving and shouting, "Good luck!" I wave back with too much enthusiasm and almost create a catastrophe. Letting go of the handlebars with one hand and waving vigorously throws me off-balance. I cannot tell you how I recover, but I do!

At 5:00 p.m. after sixty-nine miles I see with pleasure a campground. In spite of exhaustion and my painful bottom, this wonderful day and the side effects of the "Rick miracle" fill my heart with joy. I set my tent, cook the inevitable pasta, put some appeasing cream where it is hurting, if you know what I mean, and fall asleep like a baby.

Early the next morning I am ready for another great day. The sky is blue. The mountains are beautiful. I just wish that the climbing was finished. But no, *au contraire*, the road gets steeper. The temperature is not too hot yet, so in fact I reach the top with not too much difficulty. From there, I "fly" four miles downhill on a six-percent grade to the old copper town of Miami, Arizona (elevation 3,544 feet).

After a short stop, I take the SR 88, also called the Apache Trail. This trail was created in 1905, to transport supplies from Phoenix and Globe to the construction site of Roosevelt Dam. The road gets narrower and I am now on a nine-percent downhill. It is scary! I am especially afraid of cars. My speed reaches twenty-two miles per hour when my hands are on the brakes and twenty-eight miles per hour when I release the brakes. For my heavy machine and me, it is very fast.

Now I follow the road along the deep blue Roosevelt Lake, surrounded by the beautiful mountainous scenery of the lower Sonoran Desert. At the Roosevelt Dam's Visitor Information Center, I learn that I passed a campground with showers three miles back. No matter the number of miles, I want a shower! One hour later, I walk to my oasis with my towel on one shoulder, my change of clothes on the other, my mini bathroom kit in one hand and some coins in the other hand. I put enough quarters in the "box" to not run of water in the middle of my shower. It is very unpleasant to be wearing only soap and shampoo and be obliged to go out to find more coins! I do not have to tell you about NOT having enough coins... But in most cases, a well-deserved shower is a moment of paradise. The feeling of the warm water, the relaxing effect of the smell of the silky soap and the humidity of the air...hmmm.

It is now the middle of the afternoon. The air is fiery with a dry, hot wind. I decide not to go further today. I erect and attach securely the tent to a tree and the bench table, so it does not blow away. I spend the rest of the afternoon and the evening taking care of my laundry, letters, journal, and enjoying the present moment. I sit down in the shade facing the lake and think about my trip so far. The climbs are hard. I am tense when the descents are vertiginous. The heavy winds and extreme heat of the desert, like the extreme cold in Alaska, can be difficult to bear. Being alone in a foreign country and sleeping in weird places is sometimes worrisome. But despite all these difficulties, I would not change anything. I chose it, I do it, I love it. I ask myself, "Are you going to spend your life bicycling around the world?"

"Why not?"

"But there will come a time when you will grow tired of it, and you will miss the people you love back home and your country."

"Yes, I guess so. In fact my idea, since the beginning, is to experience something extreme for me, to know myself better. Maybe I will realize during this trip that I was born to bike all over the planet, or maybe I will discover the profession I am supposed to follow. Or maybe I will come to the conclusion that my old routine back home is in fact what I need. We'll see. Right now, the only thing I know for sure is that I need to change *something*. I know now that it took a long time for me to act on this feeling because I was not ready. For a long time, I was dreaming, hoping, complaining, but I did not know what was wrong or what to do about it. I only knew, vaguely, that something was not right. And now at least, I have it clear in my mind that I want to find out the truth, or rather *my* truth."

I leave the campground early the next morning and head to Tortilla Flat. At the Theodore Roosevelt Dam I see the sign: "No pavement next twenty-two miles." I am sorry to read that and at the same time I smile and tease myself, "Remember Michelle? I chose it, I do it, I love it. It is so easy to say fine words when you are comfortably resting after a nice shower, surrounded by gorgeous scenery. Now, facing difficulty, it doesn't seem as easy, does it?"

Making fun of myself, I begin the hardest and longest twenty-two miles of this trip. There are no huge ruts, holes, or rocks, like in Colorado or in the Coronado Forest, but here the distance I have to cover is greater, the road is narrower, and the traffic is heavier. Also, the deep, fine gravel makes it impossible for me to stay on the bike. The tires sink and it is as though the wheels are in chocks. The load is too heavy. I have to push very hard to go forward, and at the same time I need to lift up the bike and go up the mountain. With such treatment, I finally hurt my fragile low-back. I have been worried about that every time I have had to push Sam. I was almost confident that my back would stay strong after many dirt roads without a problem. But this time it is too much. I do not want to abort my trip again because of my health. I do not want to give up my dream. It cannot be finished so soon! "Please, my lucky star, help me again," I say.

I need to rest and stretch. I step out of the bike, which does not fall because of the depth of the sand! No...I am joking! We need some humor here. Truly, I lean the bike against a rock. Then I begin some stretching exercises for my body and some motivation speech for my head. A few minutes later, I decide to use my stubbornness and forget the pain. "I chose it, I do it and..." O.K., right this minute I do not love it, but I have to go on anyway.

I take a big breath and go back to the challenging "back test". I use my legs and arms to their maximum to save my lower back. Oh great! the road goes down. It is a short relief, because since it is still too scary for me to get on the bike, I have now to hold back the weight. Although fortunately there is less and less gravel, this is the beginning of a bumpy, corduroy-patterned downhill. It is a new challenge. I get on the bike and try to stay on it. I feel the rear wheel sliding to the left, then to the right. I really do not like this sensation. I am not a mountain-biker at all. I brake thoroughly to roll as slowly as possible on the bumps. My hands ache. I did not know that the worst is to come. It appears in the form of a huge pickup truck pulling a heavy, oversized load, including a boat and a jet ski. Earlier, I had decided to bike on the wrong side of the narrow road, since the right side was next to a steep cliff. But when this huge truck announces the start of rush hour, I begin to wonder where am I the safest? They do not expect me to be on this road, let alone on this side of it. Even if I can hear them before they arrive, and so I stop and cover my face to avoid swallowing a thick cloud of dust, I am afraid to be hurt by flying rocks and gravel.

All morning I fight with the road, the bike, the traffic, and myself. Luckily, around noon I arrive at a safe viewpoint above Apache Lake Marina, more or less in one piece. I need to rest and eat a good meal to go on this afternoon. I see the marina way down below, on the lakeside. There is no way that I could push Sam back up, if I take him down there with me, so I park him under a shelter at the viewpoint. I will pick him up when I return to the main road later this afternoon to continue on my way. So I walk down and realize that it is further than it looks. Actually, it is two miles down. I am very happy to walk light and that I left the bike behind me, because just my own weight drags me to slide and almost fall many times. I go into the restaurant. It is nicely cool inside. I close the door behind me and it is like I left the "weight" of the heat outside. I feel light and hungry. The smell of the cuisine puts water in my mouth. I order a simple hamburger with fries and salad. It is now not very original, but at the time, it was the best hamburger with fries and salad of my life. My mouth deformed by too big a piece, I am thinking, "What a morning!"

Tortilla Flat is still far away. My pace on the rough road is very slow, so after an hour of rest, I need to go back on the road again if I want to reach my destination before nightfall. I begin to walk back up to the main road when a couple with a pickup truck stop and ask me to jump in the back. I obey with great pleasure. When we reach the main road, I jump out, thank the couple, and go back to Sam. The heat is stronger than ever. I pedal, push, avoid the cars, and continue to be shaken by the "washboard" texture of the road. Every turn gives the hope that it is the last one, but every turn hides another. I keep complaining about the difficulties, but I have no regret to be here. The countryside is absolutely gorgeous. Both Apache Lake, which I passed this morning and Canyon Lake, which I am passing now, look like fjords as blue as the Mediterranean Sea. The mountains are covered with a variety of desert plants, wildflowers, the towering saguaros, and other cactuses.

The climb gets steeper. I cannot push the bike. It is too heavy. I keep sliding down. I am at the end of my tether. I decide to rest a while. The road is so narrow that it is dangerous for me to stop right here. I have to move down to a turn where there is a small guard wall. I lean Sam against the wall, sit down on it, and use my foot as a chock against the bike's rear tire, to prevent it from rolling down. There is just enough room for Sam and me to rest a while without disturbing the traffic.

From my resting spot, I look at the marvelous scenery, which always erases my fatigue, and today, my back pain too. I see the road where I came from snaking down the canyon. It is impressive. From this distance I can admire its beauty and forget its dangers. The russet walls of the canyon are covered by saguaros, ocotillos, and other cactuses.

After about ten minutes I am ready to continue pushing up the mountain. My pushing position wakes my back pain instantly. I take a deep breath and focus on how lucky I am to be here in the middle of this countryside that I like so much. But, I have a lot of difficulty moving the bike. The traffic pushes the dirt onto the shoulder, and I am literally sinking in it. I am struggling when a brand new van with four people inside stops in front of me.

The driver rolls the window down, and asks, "Do you need a ride?"

I block the bike with my foot, and answer, "Thank you so much, but I think I am not far from Tortilla Flat now."

"It is at least four miles up."

I calculate four miles...six kilometers...boy... "It is so nice of you to stop but I do not think that you have enough room for me and the bike."

"We can work it out."

Two men get out of the van and open the back doors, and inside two women hurry to make some room. I am so touched and so embarrassed at the same time to see them striving so much for me.

"Now, here we go, put your stuff in," the driver tells me.

I carry one of my bags towards the car, and I see with horror that the interior of the van is an immaculate ivory. I am tired, it is true, and fighting four miles more will be hard, but when I see all the trouble we have to deal with, I am uncertain. But these two couples seem so happy to help me that I stop hesitating and try to hurry. We cannot stay here too long. The spot is wrong. After all my baggage is loaded, I go inside and the men try to put the bike in. They push and struggle to close the door. Before I can stop them, I see the front tire make an ugly black stain on the upholstery. "Oh, I am so sorry," I say, mortified.

"No problem. Don't worry... So, where do you come from?" asks one of the women.

The two men jump in the van and we go. I am trying to find my place somehow or other, between their stuff, my stuff, the bike, and their big cooler. I tell them who I am, where I am going, what I am doing here, etc. They are on vacation from Milwaukee. I say, "In Wisconsin? I heard about Milwaukee on television in France. I enjoy Michael Landon's series, "The Little House in the Field."

"Ah! Ah!" everyone laughs. "You really have this series in France?"

"Oh, yes. I will say that sixty percent of our programming is American. Everything is dubbed in French. Did you know that John Wayne speaks perfect French?"

"Ah! Ah!" they laugh again.

"For me, American cinema and series are the best. American cinema knows how to entertain people. We have, of course, good French programs, but in smaller quantity."

"Hey, here we are. Tortilla Flat. We're going to stop here for a little while, and then drive on. Do you want to go on with us?"

"No, thank you very much. There is a campground here, so it is my stop for the night."

We put Sam and all my stuff on the sidewalk and say good bye.

Tortilla Flat is a famous authentic old stagecoach stop where only six people live. You can see the cute town in its entirety in approximately three minutes: there are a total of five old buildings that support each other from falling!

I have time, so I buy some wonderful chocolate ice cream and enjoy the rustic gift shop. Then, I sit down on a bench, and write some postcards. Around 5:00 p.m., I slowly head to the campground. The road after Tortilla Flat is a lot nicer. That feels good under the wheels! I see the campground sign and there appears to be a special notice attached on it. I get closer and read this unlucky message: Campground Closed. M---e! (English translation: S—t!) The dashes are here to avoid offending you, Reader, and also to prevent my mother from slapping me!

I have to go on. Fortunately the road is good but it is still very steep. I hope to find a place to stay somewhere along Canyon Lake. But I find nothing. Now I leave the lake behind me and the road leads to the mountains. It is magnificent and completely isolated. There is no campground or suitable place to set my tent. Happily, the non-stop climbing is finished and now I go up and down, up and down. I wonder where I am going to sleep tonight. With mixed feelings of fear and admiration, I watch the sun setting in an explosion of fabulous colors. My only choice is to go on.

A few miles further, I see the Lost Dutchman Campground. I am so happy to stop and enjoy a well-deserved rest facing the Superstition Mountains. The glowing sky gives them a warm reddish-brown color, and the shape of the saguaros stand out against the horizon. Every day the sun leaves the stage in a marvelous dramatic show.

The next morning I am back on the road very early. A few miles from the campground I stop at Goldfield Ghost Town. In the 1890's it was a booming community. It boasted a population of three to five thousand people, three saloons, a hotel, boarding houses, and a general store. There were fifty working mines in the district.

Now, two hours before the opening of the site to the tourists, I walk on the main street alone. Everything is quiet, old, rusty, and abandoned. It is fascinating to imagine thousands of people living here one hundred years ago. I saw so many "Western" movies that suddenly, I can see the street animated with miners, cowboys, horses, kids running, the owner of the general store sweeping his front porch, and the prostitutes waving from their balcony. I can hear the music from the saloon and suddenly a body is ejected through the swinging saloon doors onto the dirt outside. I look inside. Everybody punches everybody; the closest face will do. Hiding under the bar, the bartender blindly throws glasses at the battlefield. Suddenly a shot rings out. Everybody freezes, except this guy in the corner who finishes breaking a chair on the back of the nearest victim. They look at the door and see the dark shape of the sheriff standing out against the daylight, his Colt still smoking in his hand, the star shining on his chest... The scream of a crow reminds me that it is time for me to move on.

I pass Apache Junction and head to Phoenix. I have no intention to bike in downtown Phoenix, and I want to get out of the suburbs before the night, so I stay on the bike all day and pedal. It is very hot. The road is pretty flat and my lower back feels fine now. I have a good pace when suddenly in the middle of the afternoon my saddle breaks. As I said at the beginning of the story, my father put my old childhood saddle on which was not compatible with my new bike, but it was what I wanted. Until now it was great, but it finally failed. Now when I sit down on it, it rocks backwards. I have to hold it in place by attaching the front of the saddle to the frame with a scarf. It is working well, except that I have to tighten the knot every two miles!

I take a secondary road, hoping to find a safe spot to spend the night. This countryside road is infinitely more pleasant. At the end of the day, seeing nothing except fields, I ask a couple stopped at an intersection if they know of a place to sleep. They tell me about a campground four miles away. I am thrilled to hear that. Full of motivation, I bike harder, almost forgetting my usual end-of-the-day sore derriere. I pedal with enthusiasm, searching for the place, but after going more than four miles, I am tired and worried. It is seven miles further before I find the campground with delight. After traveling seventy-four miles, I fall asleep very quickly after a shower and a light dinner.

The next day, forty-one miles later, I arrive at Gila Bend. I biked all morning, stopping a thousand times to tighten the scarf that holds the saddle straight. It is particularly hot and dry today; I feel like drinking all the water in the town. I want to find a cool place to spend the afternoon to come up with a better solution for my saddle. There is no campground here; only an RV park that does not accept tents. Someone tells me, "You can pitch your tent anywhere you want outside of town—just be careful of the snakes!" I do not want to deal with snakes or anything else, so I hatch a plan to sneak into the RV park under the cover of the night and try to find a small spot for my tent.

In the meantime, I work on Sam. I put my rear tire on the front wheel and the front tire to the rear wheel because the rear weight used the tire twice more than the front. I also replace the scarf with some wire around the saddle to hold it horizontal. I wrap the scarf around the wire and cover the whole saddle with my sweatshirt. Satisfied for now with my temporary repair, I go just before dark to the RV park. I find a small spot, set my tent, and try to sleep. It is too hot.

At 4:30 a.m., I decide to strike camp. It is stormy and some lightning tears up the night sky. I wait a little bit and notice that towards the west, where I am headed, it is clearing. I decide to leave. The sky is dark and low. Finally, the rain comes, only for five minutes, but enough to get me soaking wet. Then the weather clears up quickly, and I am dry just as quickly. I decide to go until Sentinel for my middle morning stop. The road is completely flat. I am surrounded by desert valleys. There is really nothing to see. I have a good pace and my temporary saddle is working. Yet, after eighteen miles I see the Sentinel exit sign with pleasure. I am thinking, "Just a quarter of a mile and I will rest." I am biking on the shoulder and there is a truck stopped in front of me. I look in my mirror to go on the right lane of the freeway, pass the big truck, and go back on the shoulder. I motivate myself, "Almost there, just a few minutes before a cool, shady place." At the same moment, the truck passes me and blows his horn. As usual, I wave back. I am accustomed to that. So many people give me encouragement by honking, screaming, or waving. I watch the truck taking the Sentinel exit. A minute later, I am ready to do the same, but I see the truck stopped at the bottom of the off ramp. It looks like it is waiting. My suspicious mind turns on. I do not know why, but I feel trouble. I do not want to take any risk. My trip has been excellent so far. With anger, in spite of my fatigue and my desire to rest a while, I decide to go on. I pass above the truck on a bridge. My doubts disappear and my fear becomes real when I see the truck moving on and following me back on to the freeway. I feel it right behind me. It passes me and stops on the shoulder again. My heart beating hard, I pass him again, looking straight in front of me. I see in my mirror the driver making signs that I do not understand. I just go on like a pedaling machine. A few seconds later I can hear the big engine coming fast behind me. I bike on the edge of the shoulder, trying to make the most distance possible between it and me. He passes me at great speed, moving a lot of air against me, and disappears. What a relief! I am happy to not have stopped in Sentinel, but now the next exit is fourteen miles further.

I arrive at Dateland for lunch. I hope I do not find the truck here! This place is surprising. There is a gas station, a market-restaurant, and a dozen date trees. Nothing else that I can see. I eat lunch in the shade. One hour later I go back on the freeway.

I arrive at Tacna in the late afternoon. There is no campground here, so I will have to "invent" a place for tonight. I do not want anybody seeing me camp alone in the desert, so I will wait until the night to set my tent. Meanwhile, I write some letters while sitting on a bench outside the Post Office and relax. The postmistress, leaving to her home, asks me where I come from and some other questions. She tells me to ask a Basque lady, who owns the restaurant on the next street, for a place to sleep tonight. Grateful and hoping, I walk to the place indicated. A waitress from this beautiful Basque Restaurant (built in the middle of nowhere) shows me the owner's house. I knock at the door. At first the Basque lady is suspicious and tells me that she has no facilities to offer me. I tell her that I am self-sufficient and I just need a place to put my tent for the night. She finally offers me a place in her garden. I am so happy to not have to spend the night near the freeway with the coyotes and snakes.

The next morning from Tacna, my route takes me through more desert first, then through green fields in an irrigated valley, and finally through a fourteen-mile long string of RV parks to Yuma. It is just before lunch. Nothing really grabs my attention. I hesitate between staying here for the night, or going further. It is too early to stop, but the heat is incredible. The desire to go on wins.

I am approaching California. It is the 25th of September, 1 p.m. I have to stop at the border checkpoint. The border officers tell me that there is really nothing for about forty miles. They give me water, ice, and wish me good luck.

I get back on Sam and we leave the nice shade from the roof of the checkpoint. I immediately feel the heat falling on us like supplementary luggage. For several days now, I protect my skin from the fierce sun with a special outfit (designed with the resources on board) consisting of my pajamas/leggings pants, a baggy long-sleeved shirt, and scarves tied around my hands and neck. I am glad to wear my desert gear today. It must be at least 120 degrees Fahrenheit. On my right now, the Algodones Dunes. I feel like I am crossing the Sahara, not California. I am waiting to see some camels at any time!

I am still pedaling late into the afternoon. There is nothing to see except the All American Canal, which brings water from the Colorado River to Calexico for the irrigation of the Imperial Valley. I feel tired, and I see the freeway disappearing in front of me in a melting, moving mirage. I have to go on, hoping that the next exit will have a campground. Around 6:00 p.m. I see that the exit, Holtville, has one. I pedal as fast as I can, and stop at the first store to ask for directions to the campground. Nobody understands me or perhaps they do not know where it is. I do not have the courage to go on further. It is my longest day: ninety-three miles. I decide to wait until dusk, and then go set my tent somewhere out of sight.

Almost at the limit of the town, I see an open space with a sign saying that three days camping is allowed. Splendid! I decide to eat first, and then set my tent in the dark. I am just finishing my pasta when the bright lights of a car shine on me. I think to myself, "Uh! Oh! Here come problems." I put my hand above my eyes to try to see who is coming. A small man comes up to me and asks me where I come from. I answer distrustfully. He says that he is from Peru. The car's lights turn off and I see a second small person coming up. "This is my wife," he says.

"Hello," I say with relief.

"She is French," the man says to his wife.

The wife takes my hand in hers and speaks to her husband in Spanish. I am wondering when she is going to give me my hand back.

"Are you Christian?" the man asks me.

"I was baptized Catholic."

They speak together in Spanish. Finally the woman lets go of my hand and the man asks me, "Are you going to sleep here tonight?"

"Yes."

"It is not a good place here."

"Do you know a better place?"

He lifts his chest and chin proudly, and says "Yes, I own a mechanical garage. You're welcome to spend the night there. It is fenced and safe."

I think of the situation and decide to follow them. This couple seems very nice. I am glad that I do not have to set my tent here. I put my cooking stuff away, and I bike behind their vehicle for a few minutes. We arrive at the garage. The wife stays in the car while the husband shows me a small, untidy room with a desk and a sofa inside the garage. "You can sleep here. I will come back tomorrow morning," he says. I thank him at the gate, which he closes behind him. I am locked inside.

I go back to the small room. It is like an oven inside. But there is no window and no way to cool the room. I arrange my thick, warm sleeping bag on the dirty, smelly, greasy sofa. I am very tired. I need to rest. I am ready to lie down when suddenly I hear someone opening the gate outside. I go look and see the garage owner with another man behind him. I look for the wife, but I do not see her. The husband tells me, smiling, "This man needs a place to spend the night, too. He is a friend from Puerto Rico. I used to let him sleep here once in a while. I am a good Christian."

I am surprised, annoyed, and worried, but I do not know what to say. It is too late to go anywhere now. I am still wondering what to do when the Peruvian man leaves, locking me and the other man in his garage. I decide to be as calm and careful as necessary to avoid any kind of problem. I am going to spend the night locked in a filthy garage with a homeless man from Puerto Rico with a prosthesis on one leg. Can you believe that? Not even someone's imagination could invent something like that! Just in real life! "Stay cool, Michelle," I tell myself, with sweat on my forehead.

The man tries to speak to me in Spanish. Politely, but firmly, I tell him that I do not speak Spanish. I go back in "my office." He is staying in the garage. I cannot close the door because there is a mountain of paper against it, and besides, if I did I would suffocate very quickly. I begin to feel angry for having accepted help.

I lie down on the sofa and try to relax. In fact, all my senses are on the alert. The heat inside this room is hell. I am sweating like in a sauna. I do not want to move and remind him that I am here. I feel like a child frozen in his bed, thinking that a monster is hiding somewhere in the dark ready to eat him.

After half an hour of lying rigidly in the dark, sweltering cell, feeling my anger build, my worst nightmare comes true: I see the man's shape at the door. He speaks to me in Spanish. I pretend to be asleep. He stays there in the doorway for what seems like an hour to me, but is really only about a minute, I guess. Finally he goes away talking to himself. I take a deep breath of the dusty, warm air (Ugh!). I hope that he is going to sleep... Oh, no! I hear him drinking.

For about half an hour I listen to the sound of bottles on the floor. It is interesting how we do not know, ahead of time, how we will react in a dangerous situation. Instead of being afraid, as I would have thought, I am angry. Very angry. I am ready to cut him in pieces if he dares touch me! I am not exaggerating what I felt, or trying to make myself sound like a hero; I really felt like a wild animal that was just captured and locked in a cage, full of aggressiveness.

One hour later I am still lying rigidly on my back, baking in this oven, when I hear him coming up to me again. I turn my head very slowly in his direction. Oh boy! He is on his knees and entering my territory—I guess that he is in this position because he removed his prosthesis. He is crawling towards me. I stop to breathe. I do not move one eyelash, but I am thinking, "If you touch me, I will kill you." He is now near me and touches my shoulder lightly with one hand. I sit up straight, violently, and shout aggressively, "What's going on?" Very surprised at my unexpected reaction, he starts to move back. He sputters something in Spanish. I answer very roughly, "I don't understand what you say. I am tired. Go away!" He is crawling back to the door and disappears in the garage. I fall back on my sleeping bag, stiff as a broomstick, looking up in the dark, feeling my heart beating in my head. Boom-boom, boom-boom.

After my heart is back in my chest, I spend the rest of the night as rigid as a dress stand, keeping my eyes wide open and straining to hear every sound. The heat is unbearable. I am all wet from perspiration and tension. I am getting so stiff. I relax my muscles a little bit, inch by inch. I do not want to make any noise; I do not want to touch any part of the filthy sofa. It was a real nightmare, believe me!

At 6:00 a.m. I hear the metallic noise of the gate, being opened. The garage's owner does not have the time to put one foot inside that I am already at the gate my packed bike by my side. I see the surprised look on his face.

"Already up! How was your night? Do you want some coffee?"

"No. Thank you very much. I am ready to go."

"Are you sure you don't want coffee?"

"No, thank you. I need to get on the road."

"Wait here," he says, walking quickly inside the garage. I push the bike through the gate. He is back, saying,

"Please, take this Bible."

"It is nice, but I have too much weight already."

"You have the Bible in your heart," he says, smiling at me.

"Yes. Thank you and good-bye."

I am out. He follows me in the street. "If you want to wait until 9:00, I can drive you to El Centro."

"No, thank you."

I do not let him talk more; I bike away from the "Garage of Hell!"

IX

Rendezvous with Destiny

The perfume of freedom smells particularly good this morning. I did not see the Puerto Rican since our last "talk." I do not know where he was this morning and I do not want to know, ever. I thank my lucky star again. I believe I have been very lucky.

Two hours later I am doing some shopping in El Centro. It is already 80 degrees, and it is eight o'clock in the morning. It is incredible. I tell a very nice lady at the visitor center about my awful night, and ask her if there is a safe, restful place with showers close by. I am exhausted. She makes a phone call and explains to me the way to a very nice RV park where I am allowed to put my tent for one night.

I gladly go back on the road, knowing that in a few miles I will be resting safely. Why I do not get a room in a motel? Well, I tried two places in El Centro where the prices were reasonable, but still too expensive for my budget. But also, I prefer a safe place outside, in nature, to the cold air conditioning of a cheap downtown hotel.

I arrive at the RV park at noon. I made a detour (a six mile mistake...Oh well). I am entering an oasis in the desert: a marvelous green lawn, beautiful palm trees, a superb giant swimming pool. The paradise after hell. This is something I learned during this trip: after bad there is always good, after the rain, the sun, after uphill, downhill, after effort, comfort... Sometimes the bad times are long and the good times are difficult to reach, but they will get there if you allow it. Just believing is already a good advantage to finding them quicker. This is why, after a hard day and a horrible night, I am now floating all alone, on the delicious blue water of a huge swimming pool. Life is so amazing... After this restful bath of pure gratefulness and appreciation...I go take a nap! I wake up to snack in the evening, then go back to sleep until 5:00 the next morning.

It is 6:00 a.m. now and I am on the road. It is still dark. The road climbs lightly and the headwind gets stronger as the sun comes up. I pass a "town" named Plaster City where the only thing I see is an enormous factory, like a giant, dusty, industrial ghost in the middle of nowhere. I learn later that it is a drywall factory.

A few miles further I stop at Ocotillo. From here I see my route, Highway 8, going up to 4,000 feet. I try to fill myself up with all the courage, motivation, strength, and energy that I can find, and then I begin to climb. I push hard on the pedals until my legs are empty. Then I get off the bike and push hard until my arms feel empty too. It is "déjà vu."

However, today the difficulties add up. There are the wind, the heat, the dry air, the broken saddle and the load, which becomes heavier every day. It is because my tourist nature is stronger than my need to keep my load light, and my bags are filling up with souvenirs...such as colorful rocks and a chrome motorbike license plate saying "Born to ride." I had to pick it up! It is incredible what you can find on the shoulders of the roads!

Around me, the scenery is otherworldly: mountains of huge, rosy boulders piled up on top of each other...followed by *more* rocks... and *more*, all enormous as far as the eye can see. The sky is even more blue than anybody could dream. About every mile along the road there are reservoirs with water for cars' radiators. I understand why; it is so steep and so hot. It is one of those times when I wonder what I am doing here...

Exhausted, but happy, I reach the summit of Mountain Springs Pass (3,241 feet). It took me five hours. My temporary saddle fix worked; the sweatshirt did protect my derriere sufficiently to not feel the wire... From the Pass, I fly downhill and stop at a gas station, where I enjoy a well-deserved lunch. The place and the food are certainly not fancy, but I am so happy to be here that everything is great. I rest about one hour and go on toward San Diego. I am so eager to get there and take some real vacation. I will leave my stuff at a campground for a few days, and find a new saddle. With a light bike I will enjoy the weather, the scenery, the beaches, write to Rick, think about the future, and relax.

I am pedaling along, lost in thoughts, when a police car stops in front of me. I stop too, keeping my hands on the handlebars in plain sight and wait for the policeman to ask me to roll my window down! O.K., now I am joking, but at that moment I was not laughing. The officer comes to me and explains to me that in California bicycles are not allowed on the freeway. "The Old Highway 80 will take you to San Diego in a much safer and more pleasant way," he tells me. I am glad to learn of this road. I do not like the freeway obviously, but my map is for motorists and does not show the Old Highway 80. I am ready to go out at the next exit, but the officer shakes his head negatively and tells me to go back to the one I just passed. I look at him, extremely surprised, thinking, "Does he want me to cross the freeway?"

"Follow me, please," he says. Then he goes to his car, puts on the warning lights and begins to back up. Quite surprised, I turn my bike and follow him. So if you were motoring by that day, you would have seen a strange sight indeed in the emergency lane: a weird cyclist biking the wrong way on the freeway, following a police car going backwards!

When we take the exit, he shows me how to find Old Highway 80 and then drives away. I am crossing a very small town curiously named Boulevard. I do not feel comfortable here: most buildings are closed, abandoned, or falling apart. "Where is the town? Where are the people?" I ask myself.

One of the big differences I find between the U.S. and Europe is in the churches. In France particularly, every town has a church, every village, even the smallest, has its church. This is the symbol and the center of a town. If there is no church, there is no village. I need to explain here that for me a church is an old (the one in my village is 700 years old) stone construction with a pointy steeple that you can spot easily. When you find it, you know that you are in the center of the town, the place where there is *action,* because around the church will be the city hall, the elementary school, the post office, the boulangerie (bakery), the café, and the little store which sells newspapers, magazines, cigarettes, and lottery tickets among many others things. This is the soul of the village. This is something I like in France.

America is young, new, different, and full of potential. This is why the rest of the world envys you so much. The lack of churches, the way I know them, is just an observation that occurred to me when I visited and not a criticism. I know that there are a lot of churches representing many different religions in the U.S., but there are just not as visibly obvious as in France.

Back to this other, apparently "unchurched" town named Boulevard. I pedal slowly, looking around. With the wind in my face, the road going lightly up and the meeting with the police, I suddenly feel the effects of my five-hour climb this morning; I am eager to stop and find a place to sleep.

I pass a cute, little, blue building that houses the local video store and then I notice a man leaning against a white car in front of the next building, which is the Post Office. His arms are crossed. He is wearing a yellow tee-shirt, with the inscription "Use Your Intuition" on it. He is looking in my direction. Just as I pass in front of him he says, "Hello!" I look at him. He goes on, "I was waiting for you." The surprise, the curiosity, and the uphill incline stop me. "Hello," I answer with suspicion, awaiting explanations. "I saw you earlier and I was wondering how you climbed the mountains with this loaded bike. Where did you start?"

As you know, during my trip, I had a lot more good encounters with people than bad, but the worst of the bad was the night before last and I am not as friendly as usual. (Sorry, sir.)

"*El Centrro...zeess morrning.*" I answer.

"Are you French?" He asks me, smiling.

"Yes."

"Do you know a French company named Mavic? They make the best bicycle wheels in the world."

"No...sorry," I answer, embarrassed.

As I said at the beginning of the story, I am not a bicycle expert at all. I just use the bicycle to travel cheaply, to do something special one time in my life, and to be free. I feel ashamed to be so ignorant about bicycles, because I am cycling and maybe because as a Frenchman, I am supposed to know about it.

"Where are you going?" the man asks me.

"Campground Lake Morena."

"Hmm, it's far from here and I'm not sure it's a good place. You'd better take a room at the motel."

"It is not in my budget; I will be fine," I say.

I think to myself, "Here is another kind person who is afraid for me. So many people I have met along the road have been so concerned for my safety, advising me to stay in motels. It has been a surprising discovery for me to realize that both Americans and I think it is safer abroad than in our own countries. When I tell American people that I will not consider biking by myself like this in France, they look so surprised. They answer me that they think that

Europe is safer than America. I am thinking the contrary! The reality is that there are wonderful people everywhere, and danger too. You need to be careful and use your good judgment.

As I prepare to leave the man says, "I am Ralph. Here is my card. If you have any trouble call me."

"Thank you very much. Bye."

"Good luck!"

I go on my way uphill thinking that I would like to stop around here, but my "adventure" in the Garage of Hell prevented me from asking the man if he knew a place to put my tent. He seems to be a nice man. Too bad. I smile and say to myself, "Shut up and pedal!"

A few minutes later, head down against the wind, I hear a car stopping in front of me on the shoulder. Oh, my God, here is the "nice man" back. Suddenly, I think that he is maybe not so nice, and I am getting in trouble again. I am now passing near the car, feeling very nervous. Through the car window, he tells me, "I thought about the campground you are going to. It's going to take you several hours to get there. It's getting late. I know I'm a stranger, but if you want, I have a large property where you can put your tent, or a barn if you want to camp inside, or I have a spare bedroom."

I stop and think for a while. He really looks like an honest person. I am sure he has a nice family. I am tired. Hmm... I look at him and read on his tee-shirt again, "Use Your Intuition."... I smile and say, "I accept your offer."

"Great! Do you like salmon?"

"Yes."

"Wonderful. I will fix you the best salmon in California."

He explains to me the way to his house, and doing a U-turn toward Boulevard, he shouts through the window,

"You are going to meet two of the nicest guys in town!"

I watch the white car disappear. What are these two guys he is talking about? Three guys living in the same house...

Maybe there are three houses on the big property... Maybe they are weird people... No, I am not going there... It is late, he is right, I will not get to the campground before the night... Salmon sounds good... The inscription on his tee-shirt comes back once again in my mind, "Use Your Intuition" O.K., I am tired. I do not know where to put my tent. He seems nice. I am just going to take precautions.

First step: I am going back to the Post Office to show somebody my host's card and ask how to get to his house. By doing this someone will know where I went, if I "disappear." When you see me on my over-loaded bike you cannot forget me!

One hour after our second meeting, I finally arrive at the entrance of the property. As I bike up a long, unpaved driveway, I look around and see oak trees, sagebrush, manzanitas, and incredibly-shaped rocks. I am fascinated by the sight of the property and happy to finally stop, but I am also worried that I made the wrong decision. The property is very isolated. I am wondering if I should back out now while I have the chance. But I arrive to a closed gate where the biggest Doberman I have ever seen is facing me. I did not even know that such a huge animal existed! He acts like he is happy to see me...at least it looks like it. I am not afraid of dogs. I really like them. And I do not know why, but I am not worried about him at all. Through the gate I see an old, little, blue painted, wooden house on the left and a very large metallic barn. The owner of the property arrives, smiling, and says, "I thought you changed your mind. What happened?"

"Wrong road...went back to Post Office...asked a lady the way to your place."

Second step of my plan: now he knows that someone knows where I am spending the night. Ha! Ha!

He does not seem to mind at all. "Come on in!" he says joyously. I am introduced to the dog named Ruger who is really happy to see me. What a sweet dog. Nobody told him that he is big and supposed to look mean as a Doberman, because he acts like a puppy.

"Let's go to the shop," says Ralph, pointing at the metallic building. Ruger and I follow the "master" to the barn and the door opens on...bicycle heaven. Unbelievable: all kinds of bicycles, bicycle parts, bicycle tools, bicycle accessories—everything to build, maintain, and coddle bicycles. I found bicycle paradise in the middle of nowhere! Inside, I meet Sweetie the guard cat of the shop and Ralph's two friends. Lee, a tall, gray-bearded, retired submarine commander, is presently a farmer. Robert is the owner of the local video store. They help Ralph maintain the place and assist him with his work and various inventions. He is in the bicycle business, believe it or not. Twenty years ago, he got involved with bicycles. First by collecting them, then riding them as an amateur and winning a few races, and now consulting for some famous companies like Mavic and Sram (GripShift). He also was the mechanical engineer for the U.S. Cyclist Team at the 1996 Olympic games in Atlanta. It is why, when he saw me on the road, he decided to wait for me in front of the post office. He wanted to know who was this chubby boy riding the most untidy, heavy, weird bike. He tells me later that he thought that I was a boy at first, and then a baglady!

I unload completely the bike. Ralph removes the sweatshirt and the three men stay with their mouths opened, looking at the *original new* way the French install saddles!! I explain what happened with a mix of opposite feelings: embarrassment and pride. Embarrassed because my old saddle is broken, but proud with the way I fixed it. While Robert is looking for a new saddle, Lee puts Sam on a stationary trainer named the Spin Coach that Ralph invented and commercialized. A brand new, shiny-black saddle is installed in place of my poor, old, broken one. Did I see a smile on Sam's "face"?... I get on the bike, and follow orders. I feel like a race car driver stopped at the pit. While tuning Sam, Ralph teaches me about bicycles; where was he when I needed advice?

"I am glad to see that you have GripShift on your bike. They have the best customer service in the industry. Wow! Your brakes need to be changed. Do you know how to brake?" he asks me. I am thinking "Pfff, of course I know how to brake, what a silly question." But I smile and say,

"What do you mean?" He tells me, "Most people use the rear brake to try to stop quickly. In fact, they need to use the front brake. It is much more effective because the weight transfers to the front wheel when braking. The rear wheel simply keeps the bike going straight. However, when they brake with the front brake, they have to put their body weight to the back of the bike. Come and I will show you."

He takes a beautiful Softride Bicycle (I never saw before a bike with a carbon fiber beam to hold the saddle), and we walk outside to the concrete slab in front of the shop.

"Look!" he says. He gets on the bike, pedals very fast and stops abruptly using the rear brake. I see the bike sliding and leaving a black print on the cement. "Now, I will do the same thing, but using the front brake," he says. I see him moving his derriere in the direction of the rear wheel and braking hard; there is no skid mark on the slab. "You know what I mean, now," he says with a big smile on his face.

We come back inside and now he inspects my wheels. I have Michelin tires with tubes.

"How many flats did you have? The best tires for your trip are Michelin tubeless, on Mavic rims," he says.

"I had zero flats in Alaska, and ten from Denver to here." I say.

"Alaska?…Denver?…How long were you on the road?" he asks surprised.

"It is a long story." I answer.

Sam is perfectly tuned and it is time for Lee and Robert to leave. I stay alone with Ralph.

"By the way, which town are you from?"

"From a village near Bordeaux."

He looks at me astonished first, and then with a big smile he tells me to follow him. We are going to a corner of the building where I see two refrigerators. Ralph opens the door on the most incredible and prestigious collection of Bordeaux wine. Wines that I know very well by name and fame but that I certainly cannot afford and I would never have the opportunity to drink. My God, Margaux, Latour, Yquem... If my family could see that, they would fall on their knees!

Ralph says, "Wine has been my passion for thirty years. Do you want some Margaux with dinner, even if red wine isn't supposed to be served with fish?"

I cannot hide my joy to taste such a wine. "It is too much!" I say.

This morning I was fighting against the wind, the heat, the climb, and a broken saddle, wondering where I am going to sleep and when I will find a bike store. Here I am now, ready to have a wonderful dinner with first class Bordeaux wine and Sam correctly tuned. I silently thank my lucky star again.

It is getting late, dark, and cold now. I am surprised at the extreme difference in temperature here. It is an oven during the day, and a freezer during the night. "High desert," Ralph explains to me. "We are at 3,400 feet." I am so glad to be safe inside instead of somewhere on the road. I say "safe;" well, I hope I am. Frankly, I thought that Ralph had a family living here. Now I understand that he is living alone, but I do not know why I still feel safe and good.

We walk to the house now. We enter a large room called "the bike room" (as if the barn was not enough! The whole property is Bicycle Heaven.) There, Ralph studies, designs, and fixes bikes and it is where a lot of triathletes came to train. The next room contains the kitchen, the dining table, Ralph's desk, a fireplace used as Ruger's doghouse, and a huge television. There is something about this house that makes me feel comfortable. Ralph shows me the bathroom and the guest bedroom where I put my stuff; I decided to sleep in the house. I do not know when or why I took this decision. The only thing I can say is that there is *"un je ne sais quoi"* (an I don't know what) that makes me feel safe here. Ralph asks me if I want to take a shower while he fixes the dinner. I accept eagerly. Under the nice, warm water, I begin a conversation with myself.

"Two nights ago you were living a real nightmare. How can you be here tonight alone with a man and feel confident?"

"A man who likes bicycles, wine, nature, people, has a sweet cat-lady, a gentle dog, and nice friends must be a good man."

"If he is so good, why does he live alone?"

"Well...maybe he lost his family; how can I know?"

"O.K., he seems like a trustworthy man, but *be careful*. You never know."

I come back into the kitchen. It is smelling so good. Ralph finishes setting the table. I sit down waiting for him. I notice an inscription on the wineglasses. Again, I am still surprised to find a place where I can not only spend a safe night—at least it looks that way so far—but where I have also been offered a fancy dinner and had my bike professionally checked and fixed. Not to mention that this is a place where some of the best wines in the world are mollycoddled! As you can understand it is already a very special day. So when I take my wineglass by the stem and read on it: *Chateau Ste Michelle*, I cannot tell you the feeling that submerges me at this second. How can my name be on my glass? Ralph explains to me why, but it is all Greek to me. I understand four words in ten. Discovering my name on the glass makes me feel even more like I have entered the Twilight Zone.

The wonderful smell of the plate of food that Ralph puts on the table wakes me up. My stomach says to my brain, "Stop thinking, let's eat this appetizing salmon."

During the dinner I tell Ralph in a few words the highlights of my trip. He teaches me many things about wine and how to taste and drink a great wine properly. An American is teaching a Frenchman from Bordeaux about wine! The truth is that I believe most French never learn the "wine science." Wine is just a beverage that we enjoy and respect, but that's all. I want to share with you the lesson.

How to Taste a Fine Wine

To taste red wine properly,
one must use all five senses.

1. *TOUCH-hold the glass by the stem. It is the "handle" and prevents ugly fingerprints on the bowl.*

2. *LISTEN-pour slowly and listen to the music of the precious liquid meeting the crystal.*

3. *LOOK-tilt the glass above the light of a candle and enjoy the magnificent ruby color of the red wine.*

4. *SMELL-"wine" the glass by moving the wine in the glass in circles, not too fast or the liquid will spill. Then put your nose at the edge of the glass to experience the most aroma.*

5. *TASTE-repeat step 4 and take a sip. Hold you breath. Close your lips, chew the wine, salivate, keep holding your breath. Now pass the wine over your palate, swallow, exhale through your nose and experience the "bouquet."*

"Isn't fun?" Ralph tells me to use this method to enjoy the taste of every wonderful thing like a great coffee or chocolate, for example.

After a wonderful, delicious, educational dinner (while I wash the dishes—fair is fair), we talk about my family and the French company he is working for right now. Then to cap off this special evening, Ralph shows me a videocassette of a French movie that his friend, Robert, brought him today. Ralph rented it last week and liked it so much that he asked for a copy. It is a very famous movie that I missed in France. I accept eagerly to watch it. Ralph explains to me that he cannot get a television signal here so the television set is just for videos. I sit down, almost on the floor, on a funny rocking chair without feet. Ralph sits down on another one about three feet from me.

The movie is about music and a sad love story. I am really into the story and so moved by it that I have to let some tears run down my face. At this same instant I feel a hand on my shoulder that brings me back to reality. I move out of the reach of this hand as if it burnt me and show Ralph my anger for being touched and disturbed from the movie. The message is clear.

We finish the movie and begin exchanging our feelings about it. I feel so comfortable talking to Ralph—not to be touched—but just talk. The expression "French kiss" comes up in the conversation. I ask Ralph what does it mean? He is very surprised, and says, "Don't you know what a French kiss is?"

"...Well...in most of the French families, we say hello and good-bye by kissing on the cheeks."

"No, that's not what we call a French kiss," Ralph says laughing.

Again, I feel comfortable and safe here. Even when Ralph touched my shoulder during the movie, I did not feel afraid at all. I just did not like it. No feelings of anger and fear like with the homeless man in the "Garage of Hell." I am just not used to being touched. It is kind of funny when I think that kissing on the cheeks is completely normal for me but to be touched on the shoulder is strange and uncomfortable...

Ralph explains to me what a "French kiss" is. I smile and tell him that I understand, but I never heard it called this way.

From now on the conversation Ralph and I share is very special. At that moment, I wonder why I express myself so freely and so eagerly to Ralph, a complete stranger. Now, I know why—speaking in another language is like getting naked, but keeping your clothes on. What I said to Ralph this very night (even with a limited vocabulary) I would never dare say in French. To him, in English, I could speak about intimate things, like under cover. It is difficult to explain. It is strange I know, but it is the truth. The protection of another language helped me to talk freely about myself. It is also easier to reveal yourself to a stranger. He doesn't know you and there is not too much chance of seeing him again. In my particular case, three helpful elements are joined together: a stranger, a foreign language, and being abroad far from family. So, without getting red and too embarrassed, I say to Ralph, as fast as I can in my limited English, that I never kissed a boy in my twenty nine years of life... I wait for a big laugh, but at the same time I feel so light to have said it. When I think about it today, I see how risky it was to expose myself this way. My only excuse was the magic ambiance of the circumstances that I explained above.

As I hoped deep inside me, Ralph shows no mockery, just an obviously surprised face, with a gentle smile. Encouraged by the kindness of his reaction, I tell him about my childhood, teenage years, and twenties spent with my parents, grandparents, uncles, aunts, and cousins all around me: about fifty people in all and thirty-five of them living in the same village or just a few miles away! I have been in school with three of my cousins, my sister and my best girlfriend, who was my next-house neighbor since I was six years old. Then, for nine years, I was a secretary in a construction company where my father, an uncle, and a cousin worked also. It was like another kind of family, here too. Therefore, I did not have to look for "exterior" friends and did not have the need to do so.

It takes me until almost 2:00 a.m. to explain all this, but Ralph listens patiently, and helps me to find the words.

When I finish, he tells me his story, and how difficult it is for him to understand my "family world." He lost his mother at age twelve, and never had a close relationship with his father. Ralph divorced two times and his whole family is just two children. He has no idea what it is to live in a family like mine. All his relationships are with "exterior" people, contrary to me, which have always been "interior" people.

It is fascinating to exchange stories about such opposite lives. It is three o'clock in the morning when we realize that it is time to get some rest. As tired as I am, I would like to never finish our conversation; however, reality is here and I am really exhausted.

The guest bedroom is just a mattress on the floor. Ralph retires to his own bedroom downstairs. I am in the bed for a minute or so when...a one hundred twenty-pound Doberman lays down against me! I tell you, he is happy to have some company tonight! I try to push him, to pull him, but he is too heavy. I try to call him; but he do not seem to understand my French accent! Completely exhausted, I give up and stay awake the rest of the night, because he spends his night dreaming about running after some rabbits or who knows what, and kicks my back very roughly until six o'clock when it is time for him to go potty!

Even if the dog was not there, I would not have slept because I have too many exciting thoughts going around in my mind. As incredible and foolish as it is, the truth is that I do not want to go back on the bike today. I want to talk again with Ralph. But, I cannot impose like that. What is he going to think if I ask to stay a few days more? No, I have to go back on the road.

So, at six o'clock, Ralph puts the dog out and I join him in the kitchen. "Already up?" he asks me. I tell him about Ruger. He apologizes for the dog and we laugh.

"Ralph, you are up early too?"

"I did not sleep very well either. And I needed to get up early anyway because today Lee and two old friends are coming here to install an electric gate. What do you want for breakfast?"

We eat and talk for one hour and Ralph asks me, "When do you want to leave?"

"Hum... I would like to stay... Today... Is it possible?"

"Great. Do you know softball?"

"No."

"Tomorrow I am going to see my son play in San Diego. Do you want to join me?"

"Oh yes! Could we check the road I will bike on later and visit the town?"

"Sure."

"O.K. I stay tomorrow, too!"

I hope you smile, Readers, because with Ralph I act as if I had never before considered stopping here for several days. No, the thought never even cross my mind, but he asked so kindly that of course I could not refuse! It would be very, very impolite. Ha Ha. In fact, you know the truth, I am thrilled to stay longer. I thought of it during my short night. I am so happy. I like the place. I like Ralph. I have the opportunity to take the time to learn and practice English (one of my dreams), and I am going to visit San Diego with someone who knows the town. Life is wonderful. I forget "Rick of Arizona..."

Ralph's friends arrive. Lee, then Mel, Ralph's ex-company chief-engineer for fifteen years, and Karl, a welder, about my age, and master-of-his-trade. After introductions and a cup of coffee all around, we all go outside and they begin to work on the electric gate. The weather is just perfect. Ralph promised me last night three hundred days of perfect sunshine every year. I do not know if it is true, but at least yesterday and today are among his statistics. I sit down in the shade and just admire and enjoy a courteous, sprightly, friendly work team. After a quick lunch they go back to work and I go take a nap.

Again, I cannot sleep. I do not want to miss anything of this experience. Everything is so new, unusual, and special to me that I cannot shut down my mind. I try to relax for half an hour and finally go back outside just in time to witness the first try of "operation electric gate." Ralph punches in the code and the gate slides perfectly on the rail: it is a success!

The way the team works together in total harmony, respecting each other's trades and ideas, makes me feel so good. What is better than seeing a team play or work together, and win? Every one of them shows me so much kindness, attention, and friendship. They all really get to me. I like them. I will always remember this wonderful time where I felt welcome in a foreign place.

Because of them and their behavior, I feel even more safe and secure here. I am glad to have followed my "intuition" and not followed the fear. I am really happy to know Ralph. I feel that I am going to learn a lot from him. Do you know the saying, "When the student is ready, the teacher will appear?" Well, I am ready.

After the guests leave, Ralph takes me on his daily walk with the dog across his one hundred and fifty acres of virgin chaparral, fantastically-shaped rocks, and other vegetation. The granite rocks turn purple, pink, and golden with the sunset. I smell sagebrush and some other delicate, pleasant odors that I am not familiar with. We leave the trail and climb to the highest rock of the property, from which Ralph shows me the limit of his land. The house is almost invisible from here. We sit down and enjoy the view, the sunset, and two Red Tail Hawks. They glide from one current to another, light and free. One of the most beautiful and intense symbols of nature and freedom for me is to hear the squeal of birds of prey. It just goes straight into my soul... Here, on this rock, is the pinnacle of a wonderful day.

We come back to the house in the silence of the evening twilight. After another great dinner, Ralph goes behind me and I feel his strong hands massaging my shoulders. I never experienced this before. "Boy, you are tense," he says. I do not answer, but I think to myself, "Of course, I am tense. I do not feel comfortable with you touching me like that, but at the same time it is *sooo goood*!" So, like a shy child who is afraid to play with other kids but at the same time would love to try, I do not move, I simply wait.

After a few minutes, which feel like seconds, Ralph stops the massage and asks me if I want to see "Immortal Beloved," a movie about Beethoven. I accept with joy. I have never seen a movie completely in English before. In France, late at night once a week, there is an American movie with French subtitles, but all the rest of the American movies, TV series, and shows are dubbed in French. So for me, Clint Eastwood, John Wayne, and Marilyn Monroe speak French perfectly!

From the dining table we go sit on the funny chairs like yesterday and we watch "Immortal Beloved." I do not understand eighty percent of the dialogue, but I can follow the story and appreciate the music. At the end Ralph explains to me the details I missed and we begin, again, a long and interesting conversation about the movie, about life, about death, about love. I am swimming again with delight in this sheltered, restful, intimate atmosphere. We get up and walk to the kitchen. And like this, simply, Ralph asks me if I want to try a kiss.

Instead of being offended, afraid, or any kind of reaction that I would expect from me in normal times, I look at him for an instant, speechless. For the first time, my brain shuts down for a few seconds and then it is the opposite phenomenon: many thoughts cross my mind at the same time. I must look like an idiot. Is it said that when you do not say "no" that must mean "yes"? I guess, because I stay standing up stiff as an ironing board watching his face coming close to mine. I close my eyes and present him a tightly closed mouth. So in fact, Ralph kisses me where my mustache would be, if I had one. And the only thing I feel is his mustache tickling my nose. Here is my first kiss experience, folks! I open my eyes and Ralph says, smiling,

"We need some practice here! Do you want to try again?"

"...No, thank you... I think I am ready to go rest."

"...Yes, it is late again... Good night."

I close the bedroom door—no dog tonight; I want to sleep. After about one hour of confusing emotions, I pass out for a few hours.

When I wake up in the morning, I hesitate to get up. I am afraid to join Ralph in the kitchen and at the same time eager to go talk to him. Finally, my stomach speaks and the rest follows! Ralph is fixing breakfast. He looks very happy. We wish a good morning to each other. I do not want to talk about "our kiss" because it is still confusing for me. I guess Ralph understand that because he does not say a word about it. He asks me if I am ready to go to town. I give him a big smile of relief and of joy to join him in San Diego.

He looks at me and asks me if I have other clothes than the ones I am wearing. I look at me and realize that I cannot meet Ralph's son and go to a restaurant with my clownish outfit or my old "pyjamas." I look at Ralph in dismay, and say, "No nicer clothes."

After breakfast we drive west on Highway Eight to San Diego. We are going up to 4,000 feet to drop now slowly across the mountains of Cleveland National Forest. I can see the beautiful scenery of El Capitan Reservoir. It is gorgeous! Then we drive across a San Diego suburb.

Everywhere there are palm trees, bougainvillea, and a lot of other colorful vegetation. It is so pleasant, unlike many other typical big cities. Then near the ocean it is just marvelous. San Diego County and me, it is love at first sight!

We stop at a mall where Ralph takes me to a women's clothes store. He talks to a saleswoman and he sits down waiting until I show him the result. We agree on jeans and a nice polo shirt that he buys for me. I do not know what to say, or what to think. The only person who bought clothes for me (except me) is my mother. All this is completely crazy but I cannot explain why it also feels completely normal. We act like we have known each other for years. Ralph takes care of me and I accept gladly. I am being bombarded by so many new feelings, which are opening up an unknown, but exciting new world.

Later, while Ralph is doing his own shopping, I call my mother. The routine during my "bike adventure" has been to phone my parents on Sundays and my grandparents on Wednesdays. This way, they know approximately where I am during my trip and if I am still alive. Today, I tell her that I stopped in a small town between El Centro and San Diego, that I am staying with a very nice man, and that everything is fine and I am safe. I describe the place and what I did since last Wednesday. Then I join Ralph and we go see his son, Danny.

During the drive to the softball field, I surprise myself thinking that maybe Ralph wants to introduce me to his son for another reason. I mean Danny is single and I am too. For the first time since I met Ralph I feel bad and disappointed. I wonder why I take all this so seriously, why I feel so ridiculously happy and light for two days and now so sad. The little voice inside me says, "Come on, don't hide the truth. You are, maybe, inexperienced but you are not stupid. Don't you see what's going on here?" I feel the answer coming... "I am in love with Ralph! No, that is crazy...

whoa! Wait a second here, this guy is really nice, is kind to you, listens to you, is a real gentleman—it is easy to be infatuated in this ambiance. But that means nothing. Enjoy your time here and be ready to go back on the road."

The car slowing down to park brings me back to reality. Ralph and I go sit down on the stepped rows of seats and watch the game that has already begun. Ralph points out his son proudly and tells me how wonderful he is and the real friendship they share together. Danny is really a good baseball player and a lifetime golfer. Ralph tells me how tickled he is to have given a lifetime passion to his son. Ralph introduced golf to Danny at five years old. Danny never stops practicing. He has enjoyed playing it ever since then.

The game finished, Danny comes toward us, hugs his father and smiles at me. Ralph introduces us and takes us to a restaurant. During lunch he tells his son about me and my trip. They try to explain baseball to me but I must say it is difficult for me. We laugh a lot and finally decide that we will try later. Danny seems very gentle, sweet, calm, shy, and very smart, and, I suspect, he knows more French than he wants to admit. After lunch he has to leave. Ralph asks me what I want to do.

"I am a tourist, Ralph, can you take me to what is interesting to see in San Diego?"

"I am not a tourist; I really don't know what to show you... Hum... I guess Balboa Park will satisfy your tourist appetite."

"Thank you, Ralph, I follow you."

We pass over the 400 foot long Cabrillo Bridge built in 1914 and it leads us into Balboa Park. The park was the setting for the 1915 Panama-California Exposition, and later, the 1935 California Pacific International Exposition. We walk around this delightful site. I take pictures and suddenly Ralph takes my hand and says, "Let's go see the Aerospace Museum."

Ralph's first passion is aerodynamics. He spent his teenage years building and learning about model airplanes, until winning the National Championships. Later he became a pilot. Then he got interested in bicycles, and designed one of the first modern aerodynamic bikes, known as the ZIPP Bike.

But let's go back to him taking my hand. I feel so embarrassed, but again (as with the massage) I do not move and accept. Also, I wonder why he does that. As I said above, it is like we have been friends for years. But I know it is not true, we have only known each other for three days! Confusion piles on top of confusion, I decide to just learn and enjoy the present moment.

After the visit to the museum we have to go home because it takes more than one hour to drive back. Slowly we leave the lights of the city behind, and, as we climb the mountains of Cleveland National Forest, it feels like we are driving up into the vast, starry sky above. What a show! By the window, for the first time in my life, I can see the Milky Way very distinctly. Outside: millions of bright stars; inside: the few lights of the dashboard, and beside me in the dark, the shape of Ralph's reassuring presence. I feel like I am flying in a spacecraft across the cosmos. It is so strange, so peaceful, and so easy too. Just being there. For a few minutes I am floating in the heaven of no confusion.

X

My Road to Happiness

We arrive at home. I look up; the Milky Way is even brighter here. Ralph tells me, "Boulevard's sky is the best day and night. And wait until you see our silver moon." We go inside. I go take a shower while he fixes dinner. I come back and sit down to eat. Ralph comes close to me, puts his hand on my shoulder and says that he saw me in the shower.

There is nobody a mile around the house, so the exterior wall of the shower was built as a big window, and even though the hard water leaves a film on the glass, you can still see through it. I feel hurt by his words and when he kneels down near my chair to be face to face and get a little bit closer, I say, "I think it's enough for today." Ralph gets up, goes and sits down on his chair, and begins to eat.

We exchange a light conversation about the day. Instead of suggesting that we watch a movie after dinner, he tells me that it was a long day, and he is going to take a shower and retire. I agree. I need to rest too. After washing the dishes, I go in my bedroom and lay down. I hear him in the bathroom and then going down to his own bedroom. Then, it is the silence of the night, interrupted just by some coyotes.

Thousand of thoughts bombard me. Ralph watching me take a shower, I did not think he would do this...then talking to me about it, how weird. I am so disappointed. I like him, but it is time to go away. I am agitated, confused, and sad. I cannot figure out what is going on. All night I try to sleep, but it is impossible, I am too nervous. I wait with impatience for the morning.

Finally, Ralph's footsteps resonate in the stairs. I give him a few minutes, then join him in the kitchen. He welcomes me politely and invites me to sit down for breakfast. I feel very uncomfortable. When he finally sits down, he says to me, "When do you leave?"

I am hurt, sad, completely lost. I would like to cry. I look at him and ask, "Did I do something wrong?"

I do not know why I say that, but it is stronger than me. For the first time this morning, Ralph looks me in the eyes and says with irony in his voice, "No...it's enough for today."

I stay without a reaction for a few seconds, and then all the bad feelings and my confusion make sense. I knew something was not right last night after I said that. Staying nervously awake all night was a sign.

"Ralph...I didn't like you watching me take a shower."
I see his face change from some contempt to total surprise, and he says, "I didn't watch you in the shower. I wouldn't do that! I..."

"You told me about seeing me through the shower's window..."

"I said that if it would make you feel better, I will cover the outside shower's window."

"Oh, Ralph, I am sorry, I did not understand you correctly. I spent a horrible night..."

"Me too, I didn't sleep at all. Why didn't you come and talk to me?"

"I wouldn't dare come in your bedroom! Why didn't *you* come to talk to me?"

"For the same reason as you... Michelle, please tell me when you do not understand, or when it's making no sense. We hurt each oth..."

Pushed by an incredible emotion, half-smiling, half-crying, I come close to Ralph. He opens his arms and I rush inside them, like running into a warm, friendly home to escape the ice storm outside.

"Yes, Ralph, I am so sorry."

He holds me tighter. Oh God, I would like time to stop right now, to feel forever this moment of complete well being. I am just learning about life, discovering for the first time what love is and from this minute, my life will change completely. I know it already.

It is a strange experience, to have your emotions change from one strong feeling to its complete opposite in the space of a few minutes. I was nervous, sad, confused and in an instant I am peaceful, happy, in love, loved...

The misunderstanding pushed me to realize how much Ralph's behavior already affects me. If he smiles, I am happy. If he is sad, I am miserable. Also, it pushed me to show my true feelings. Feelings that I was hiding from myself too. I knew that I was falling in love with Ralph, but I was so afraid by my inexperience that I was trying to gain time until... I do not know when... I am glad about this misunderstanding because it allows us to express the truth. And the horrible night we spent going our own separate ways was not for nothing.

"Let's finish our breakfast now," says Ralph with a smile.

I love his face. I love when he smiles, when I can read kindness, joy, and now...love.

We finish our breakfast and the phone rings. Ralph has to work now. He works at home. He is an engineer, inventor, and consultant. As I said earlier, he has been a champion model airplane racer, a pilot of real airplanes, and also a motorbike rider, a bicycle racer, and a marathoner. He created and sold a successful company that builds electric motors. Lately he got awards for the design of the revolutionary ZIPP Bicycle. As you can see, Ralph is not bored or boring; he is always in search of learning, having fun and also, of course, making a living.

While he is working with Robert, Lee and "the phone," I decide to clean the house, because a bachelor's standards are not the same as a female's. If you know what I mean! In fact, it isn't so bad. The main problem is not Ralph's fault, it is the dust. We are in the high desert surrounded by rocks and the wind blows the decomposed granite everywhere.

After doing my best to clean the house, considering the local conditions, I ask Ralph if I can jog to the Post Office. He answers that the road is not appropriate for jogging because of the eight wheelers. I need to be extra careful.

While I was cleaning I decided to find a public phone to call my childhood best girlfriend for advice. I put on my tennis shoes, my cap, and head to Boulevard's "downtown." Indeed, the road isn't made for joggers. I forgot the hills, the wind, and the heat. A few days in the comfort of a house and I forgot the rough life of outside adventure!

I arrive at a public phone and dial my friend's number. The phone rings and rings. Nobody. Well, destiny is destiny. I guess this is a sign that I have to work it out by myself.

I come back "home" and fix a salad for lunch. I visit with Ralph between his business calls. Then I go sit down in the living room on one of these funny, feet-less rocking chairs. I need to rest and think some more. Suddenly I feel the chair rocking backwards. I open my eyes and try to keep balance, but my legs are already up. Ralph's face is near mine, and he says, "Do you want to begin your first real kissing lesson?"

I do not have time to say a word, just close my eyes and feel warm, soft lips on my mouth... Ralph's smile became a kiss... I open my eyes, the smile is back... "I like it... do it again," I say quietly.

The smile becomes a laugh and a kiss again. My heart is jumping out of my chest. I can hear it beating in my ears. I get a wonderful, long, kissing lesson.

"Now, it is like everything else: to improve you need to practice, practice, practice," says Ralph, laughing. "Let's go for a walk and start an early evening."

He lets the chair come back to the normal position slowly. I am still under the spell of what happened. Ralph has to help me get up and we go outside. Everything is perfect: the weather, the temperature, the smell of the vegetation, and some blue birds flying by. Is this paradise? We walk quietly, just enjoying to be together.

In the evening after dinner, the CD player plays a song I really enjoy. Ralph asks me if I want to dance. I accept eagerly. It is so good to be back in his arms again. His deep, soft voice whispers in my ear, "Do you want to practice some more?" I look at him smiling, showing my agreement. We exchange a long kiss, and Ralph says, "I love you."

"Oh, I love you too, Ralph," I say, tightening my arms around his neck. We stay an instant like this, holding each other...

"I am going downstairs. If you want I can massage your shoulder again. I will wait for you down there, Michelle, just a massage if you want...don't be worried."

He goes in his bedroom and I stay here for a while. What a weird moment. I am tempted, but scared. What to do?... Ralph's voice comes up to me, "Are you coming?" Like the voice of sirens, I feel attracted. Coming down slowly, step by step, I repeat to myself, "Just a massage, just a massage." The stairs are too short. I arrive in the bedroom too soon. I am ready to rush back up as fast as I can but I hear his voice again, saying, "Don't be afraid, I said just a massage and after you decide what you want to do. Come here and lie down." I obey. Ralph puts his hands on my shoulder and laughs,

"You really do need a massage, relax, it's O.K. Trust me."

I let go just a little bit. I cannot appreciate the massage because I do not feel comfortable on Ralph's bed.

Finally, he stops, and says, "You can leave now if you want."

I hesitate—afraid to destroy our "story" before it really begins—but I am even more scared to stay. I hear myself say, "I am not ready yet."

"I understand, it is fine, good night, my dear," he smiles at me kindly.

Lying on my bed this night, I cannot find sleep. I want to stay here, live with him. I have so much to learn, so much to experience, but everything is going so fast. We have known each other for just four days! How can we say that we love each other after four days! It is ridiculous. We act like teenagers... But what about the policeman pushing me through Boulevard at the same time as Ralph, what about Ralph's bike interest, his Bordeaux wine passion, the French movie arriving the same day, the wine glass with my name on it...and...the way I feel. Is it not incredible? Is it not a sign?... Well, you know what? I want to take it like it is a sign. A sign that destiny led me here and allowed me to let a miracle happen. I know somewhere deep inside me that I can be happy here, that I found what I was looking for, without knowing what it was. Exhausted by all the new emotions of the last days, I sink into dreamland.

Ralph's voice speaking on the phone wakes me up. It is almost 11:00 a.m. I arrive in the kitchen when he hangs up.

"Hello there! How do you feel this morning?"

"I feel *grreat*," I answer, stretching my arms above my head.

"I have some wonderful news! The French company that I work for wants me to represent them at Ironman."

"What's Ironman?"

"That's the famous triathlon in Kona."

"Kona?"

"Kailua-Kona in Hawaii, the Big Island."

"HAWAII?" I scream, with the travel fever invading me all over.

"It's a last minute project. Ironman is in three weeks and as you can imagine, it's going to be difficult to find transportation and a hotel. We'll see if it's meant to be. Hum...by the way...do you want to come with me?"

"Come with you? YES, YES, YES!"

I am so excited at the idea of going there. From France, it is so far, so expensive. I cannot wait to know if it will happen. In the middle of the afternoon, Ralph tells me that the impossible is done. He found two seats in a plane and a place to stay. I cannot keep my joy inside. I jump to his neck and give him kisses on the cheeks, and say "When? Ralph, when?"

"Let's see..." He looks at his notes. "Well, the seventeenth of October at 7:00 a.m. from San Diego."

My heart stops. I am floating in unreality. Ralph, worried, puts his hands on my shoulders as if he is going to shake me to bring me back to life.

"What's going on, Michelle?"

I am in shock. I open my mouth to repeat, "I cannot believe it. I cannot believe it."

"What? What?" he says.

Coming back to earth I explain, "Ralph, it is my birthday!"

"What?" repeats Ralph, confused.

"I was born the seventeenth of October at exactly 7:00 a.m.," I answer with tears in my eyes.

"I cannot believe it."

"That's what I said!"

I run to show him my passport. If that is not a sign, if that is not a miracle, then I am a tough believer! Ralph looks at the date on my passport, and says,

"Fascinating...fascinating."

This last coincidence is why I decided to write about my story. It is so wonderfully crazy that I want to share it with everyone.

During the three weeks before leaving to Kona, Ralph becomes obviously impatient to teach me more about "love," if you know what I mean: stop talking about it and let's do it! I let my fear control the situation a while but

I know that I cannot go on acting like a child any longer. We are in the same house and even more, in the same room, alone ninety-five percent of the time for days. So what has to happen, happened. I follow Ralph for a massage in his bedroom and this time I stay with Ralph and we attempt our first sexual intercourse.

We have some trouble getting me relaxed. I really love Ralph and I thought that when you love someone everything goes by itself naturally. But I guess, because I begin to play late at this game, my body and mind need time to adjust. It is not easy to speak about intimate things, but I want to tell how patient and loving Ralph is. It is why, instead of pressing me, getting impatient or frustrated, he reassures me; we talk, joke and laugh until I am less tense, then we try again. I feel some pain and finally loose my virtue. The pleasure I get from this first time is not physical, but spiritual. A door opens on another reality, another vision of life. A door that I thought was locked forever, because nobody would have the key.

Life is so amazing! I decided to take a six-months break to do something special in my life, to have time to think alone, to find my road to happiness. I never dreamed that it would be the road to love. I never dreamed that it would be so thrilling to feel the human contact of the person I love against me... I see the blood stain on the sheet as the sign that I belong here. Ralph holds me, and says, "I am sorry to hurt you; we will learn together. Remember: practice, practice, practice!" We laugh. I feel so fortunate to begin my education with someone experienced, patient, wise, kind, and loving. I am ready to learn how to enjoy completely my relationship with the man of my life.

The next day we drive back to San Diego to go grocery shopping. Ralph turns into a mall and parks the car. I look around, looking for a grocery store, but Ralph takes my hand and we enter a jewelry store. Without a word Ralph gives three diamonds to the jeweler, and asks him to mount one on a ring and the two others on earrings. I look at Ralph, very surprised. "Pour moi?" He puts one arm around my shoulder and squeezes me against him, and says "Yes, for you." At that moment I do not realize the value and symbolism of his act. It is too much. He explains to me, "Twenty years ago I made enough money to invest in a few diamonds. I want you to have them, to show you that I love you and to show your family that I am serious."

My inexperience and my naiveté make me think that I do not need such a gift. My family will know that Ralph is serious and they are going to be happy for me. But Ralph knows life and knows that my parents will be shocked and worried for me, so a gift like this will perhaps reassure them that their beloved daughter met a gentleman.

In the middle of the afternoon we are back in Boulevard. We go for a walk with Ruger and after dinner we try again to make love. I am eager to try again, but at the same time it is even more difficult than the first time, because the fear of pain makes me very tense and being tense obviously doesn't help. Again Ralph has to use all his patience to relax me. I know, I know for a French girl, I am not equal to the reputation! As I say to Ralph later, "Give me some time to learn and adjust and I will become an expert. You will not regret being patient." He laughs, holds me, and tells me that he loves me, no matter what.

Later the same night we are talking about traveling. I am passionate about it. Ralph is a lot more cautious.

"Ralph, you're an engineer, don't you want to see for example, the incredible Pyramids?"

"Do you want to sleep in a Pyramid?" says Ralph looking at me straight in the eyes.

"What?"

"Do you want to sleep in a pyramid?"

"What do you mean, Ralph?"

"We have a reservation at the Luxor, in Las Vegas, next week-end!"

"What are you talking about?" I say, jumping on Ralph and tickling him.

Ralph tells me that this weekend we are going to Las Vegas to meet his daughter, Patty. She is living near San Francisco with her husband, Ron. She is an executive in a Northern Californian human resources company. Ron is a very talented, famous painter. They are in Las Vegas for an art show. It is perfect to meet there.

I want to know Ralph's daughter, but also I am intimidated to meet her. I am sure you have understood that Ralph is older than me. I wonder what reaction Patty is going to have toward me. I am not sure how I would react if it was my father who would introduce me to his young girlfriend. As a matter of fact, until it happened to me, I was critical of couples consisting of two people from different generations. It is relatively ordinary, but I never understood how different generations can have things in common. How a young girl can love an older man, or a young man an older woman. It never made sense to me. Now ironically, I am in this situation and I am so ashamed about my ignorant prejudices. It is a good lesson for me. I promise myself to never judge or condemn anybody again, especially about love, because I know now, it is true that love is blind and has no age.

On Saturday morning we fly to Las Vegas and in the afternoon I meet Patty and Ron. They are very nice and friendly, amused by my accent, and maybe surprised by my manner (I do not look like a showgirl trying to seduce an older man). We have an excellent evening, except for Ralph who has a lower back problem. He has difficulty walking.

After dinner we come back to our "pyramid." Ralph spends an hour in the Jacuzzi and then I massage him to sleep (lucky guy!).

The next morning Ralph is still suffering and has to walk slowly. We join Patty and Ron for breakfast and Ralph asks Patty what she thinks about her dad with a French girl.

Patty smiles, "You're all right, Dad. There is just one problem...I won't call her Mother!" We all laugh. I feel so happy to be accepted. Ralph goes on, "In fact I don't know if she is going to stay with an old man with a broken back." I kiss Ralph on the cheek and whisper in his ear, "I love you no matter what."

The three weeks before leaving for Hawaii pass very quickly. Ralph takes care of his back. We have to get prepared for the trip. We are learning how to live together. Every day is an experience. I am in a crazy spiral. Everything is going so fast since I met Ralph. My life has completely changed already. I am in love. I, the suspicious French, find everybody nice and beautiful. All the people I meet (friends, inhabitants of Boulevard, strangers at the super-market), smile at me. I realize now that they are smiling at me because I am smiling at them. Like a wonderful sickness, my happiness is contagious. Instead of being invisible, not looking at anyone or showing a worried face that says, "Don't talk to me," I am looking at people with no fear and carrying a big smile that says, "You are all wonderful."

One of the most awesome and sweet people that I met in Boulevard is the post-mistress, Pat. She tells me how delighted she is to see Ralph and me so happy together. Her face and her smile are so honest and intense when she speaks to me. She really makes me feel good. She is like an angel blessing our love. What a friend!

As I said earlier, during my bicycle adventures I used to call my grandparents on Wednesdays. My family knows where I am, but I do not want them to be worried. My grandmother answers the phone, obviously happy to hear from me. I tell her about our trip to Las Vegas and the coming one to Hawaii. She listens to me and my enthusiasm and finally asks me with a concerned voice, "Michelle, this man seems nice but don't you think you will have to 'pay'?"

"Oh no, no Mamie, I have already 'paid'..." I say, and we laugh on the phone.

On the seventeenth of October we land in Kona. I stop a few seconds on top of the plane stairs, realizing that, yes, I am in Hawaii, it is not a dream. I follow Ralph to the exit. I feel a warm breeze, and smile when I see people with beautiful flower necklaces around their necks—like I saw it many times on television. We take a taxi and ride toward Kona.

Even knowing that the Hawaiian Islands are volcanic, I am surprised by the desert black lava ground. Then along the road to our hotel, I can read on this black background some "graffiti rocks." People write their name or a loved one's name with pieces of white corral. When we arrive at our hotel I organize our stuff for the two weeks, then we walk to my birthday dinner. I will never forget the mix of smell and color of the plumeria, gardenia, hibiscus, bougainvillea, palm trees, all the luxurious green vegetation, and the sunset.

Ralph takes me to a very nice restaurant.

During this romantic dinner I feel my heart bursting with joy, thinking that instead of celebrating my thirtieth birthday alone on some roadside, I am dining tête-à-tête with the man of my life under the Hawaiian skies. I have a lot of imagination, but I would never dream this could happen to me. I would like to scream to everyone how much I love Ralph, how great life is! After this unforgettable evening we go back to the hotel to get some rest (wink, wink, nudge, nudge!).

The week before Ironman, Ralph installs a banner on our balcony advertising the wheel company he came to represent. The day of the race, I see for the first time live what a triathlon is. What supermen and superwomen! What a challenge for mind and body! Can you believe they swim 2.4 miles, jump on a bicycle and ride for 112 miles, park the bicycle and then run a 26.2 marathon??! It is just incredible!

We follow the race, taking pictures and giving encouragement to "our" guy riding "our" Company wheels. How wonderful to see him be the first to pass the finish line!

Between Ralph's work, me visiting the Island, and a beautiful sunset every evening, we are practicing, practicing, practicing (if you know what I mean). It is still difficult for me, but I am learning every time a little more about lovemaking. Many times, Ralph shows that he is concerned I will want to return to my country. "In France you are going to find a young Frenchman and forget me," he says. I keep promising that I will come back to him. Ralph cannot believe that he is the man I want and that he is giving me what I want.

Too fast, our Hawaii vacation is finishing. I wish I will be back one day to this paradise. We come back to Boulevard and two days later I need to return to France because of the expiration of my visa. It is difficult, but at the same time I am eager to share my happiness with my family, quit my job completely, rent my home, give my car to my parents, come back to Ralph and begin my new life.

I am supposed to spend Christmas with my family and come back sometime in January. But, I miss Ralph so much that I come back in the middle of December. As Ralph expected, my parents and grandparents are shocked. They are sad to see me leave France and live so far away. Being in love makes me so happy, so insane that I do not see their pain and I even feel hurt about their reaction. Now, I realize how difficult it was for my parents to "lose" me.

So after a month in France, and a scary phone bill, I come back to Ralph with a new three-month visa. We spend Christmas and New Year's together like alone on an island. I improve my English slowly. Everything is so new. Everything is an effort. I am bombarded with a lot of new information that I have to assimilate—some completely new, some very basic. New habits are the most easy to learn because of no prejudice—no unlearning process. The basic ones, those I have known since I was a little girl, are very difficult to erase and change. I have to adapt to nine-hours time lag, a new country, a new language, a new diet, a new house, new habits, new rules, new friends, a spouse, and a sex-life. Every night I go to bed with headaches. Every night, also, I go to bed with Ralph. This is a completely new habit. I see you smile now and think: headache + be in bed with Ralph: uh! oh!, problem!

As I said earlier, I want to write about my adventure because of "the magic" of it, but also I want to share my experience of being loved by a wonderful man. So my daily evening headaches are just another opportunity for Ralph to help me, be kind to me, and love me.

From a sheltered, but spoiled girl, I am learning to be a wife. It is especially difficult when we happen to fight. I did not know men and women could be so different. Our differences are not just sex, but culture, education, generation, and language. So at first our love is often put to the test. Ralph and I know without a doubt that we love each other and consequently, it is not thinkable that we will hurt each other on purpose. But because of our differences (Ralph has a male point of view, I have a female point of view) we have fights in spite of all the love, the respect, and our bulletproof rules of communication.

Ralph and I make an agreement that we will always say the truth to each other. How many spouses do you know who keep small, painful details and bad feelings inside? They do not say what they are really feeling, either because they hurt too much or because they are afraid, or because they feel so unworthy that they think they deserve to hurt. Often some will answer by trying to hurt back. So when Ralph says or does something that hurts me, I try to keep cool and tell him in a loving way what I feel. Sometimes, I cannot talk to him just after the hurt, or I feel the hurt later, but I always talk to him about it again lovingly. Sometimes it happens that I do not realize *why* I am hurting at the time that Ralph says or does something, so I take some time to think about why I feel disturbed. It usually does not take too long to figure out what is the problem, and then I speak to Ralph about it. He does the same when I hurt him. Of course, to be a complete success, each spouse has to play the game honestly. One listens and the other talks. In a real loving situation, his or her feelings are just simply different and the intention is not to hurt the other, so usually the listener is surprised to have hurt.

I am learning all this "wisdom," not from theoretical books, but from our fights. Ralph is an experienced man and I fight him a lot at first. I am afraid to lose my personality if I obey his rules. But in fact, every game has rules, and life is a game. When you play in a team, you have to know your strategic place to be in position to win. You need a pilot to fly an airplane and a co-pilot to navigate; otherwise you can easily see that the plane will crash. It is recommended to figure out in advance who is going to do what!

Another agreement Ralph and I make is to tell each other when something is *right* as well as when something is wrong. How many people do you know who will never miss the opportunity to tell you when something is wrong, but say nothing when things are right. It is good to know where you made a mistake because you learn from it, but would it not be great to learn also when others appreciate your actions? Especially the ones who count?

These two rules of communication (truth and appreciation) are very important for us. They nourish our love. We throw away every bad feeling before it is spoiled and learn, day by day, each other better. It is a daily "work" to love and live with someone. I thought naively that when you find your "other half," love makes everything perfect and people who divorce did not find the right one yet. I know now that you have to make a common effort. Real love is this effort. I have just begun my education, but I am fortunate to love an experienced, wonderful man.

As I said earlier, I have a three-month visa and then I have to be back in France again. To be able to live with my beloved, we have to get married. Three more months is short to be sure that we are not making a mistake. Ralph has been married two times already and did not plan to try a third time. I have never been married and thought that I will never be. We are together twenty-four hours a day, but still! During each fight, we think that we are crazy to try. After each fight, we never want to be apart.

Three weeks before I am supposed to leave the United States territory, I become worried that maybe Ralph does not want to get married again because he does not speak about it. We have a good relationship and as I say, good communication, but in this case I do not know how to bring up the subject. I do not want to push him. I cannot say, "By the way, darling, when are you going to marry me? Remember, we have an expiration date!" So I wait, wondering if Ralph is going to talk to me. But he says nothing. Finally, twelve days before the deadline, I finally remind him that we need to do something about our future. He says, "Do you want to stay with me and be my wife?"

"Oui!" I say.

The same day we go get a marriage license, and to buy me a dress. Ralph invites by phone his children, and the friends I already met. Five days later, on a sunny Sunday, we are married by Arnie Baker, a good friend of Ralph's. Arnie is a medical doctor who retired to realize his cycling passion with his wife, Gero. He is now a U.S.A. cycling coach, multiple National Champion, and record holder. My destiny is really related to the bicycle—I met Ralph because of the bicycle, and we get married by a famous coach and cyclist. *"Vive la bicyclette!"*

The only thing sad for me about the wedding is not having my family for the event. Fortunately, my new family is here. Ralph's daughter and her husband come from San Francisco (on four days notice) and spend the weekend with us. For this, especially, I want to thank Patty. She is so kind, so helpful, so loving. She understands me. Secretly, I would like some flowers and Ralph is busy organizing a twenty-five persons party. I do not know where or even how to phone for flowers. I am afraid to ask. But Sunday afternoon when we arrive at San Diego to Arnie's house, Patty gives me a beautiful bouquet. It brings tears to my eyes every time I think of it. She also attaches a white carnation to her dad's boutonniere. It is so reassuring to have a friend like her when getting married in a new country, far from home, and with her Dad! Patty, her husband, Ron, and her brother, Danny, give me so much affection, support, and love. I will never forget.

After our wedding, we begin the process of filing papers with the immigration office. It takes me three years to be officially allowed into the United States. It also takes me more than two years to adjust and feel at home in this new country. The stress from my new life fighting against the old one slows down the growth of the new Michelle, especially sexually—for almost two years I have difficulties. Being tense makes me sore. Being sore, or being afraid to be sore, makes me tense. It is a vicious circle. It is Ralph's love, patience, and knowledge that helps me to overcome my fear and discomfort. I am eternally grateful to him. Day after day, by love, fight, joy, pain, fun, positive stubbornness, and communication, I learn to be the happiest wife.

Ralph has had trust and patience to break my cocoon, to teach me how to fly, and to show me that I could be a smart, pretty butterfly instead of a common, hiding caterpillar. This metaphor is, in fact, not so far from reality because I lost twenty-three pounds in three years (slowly, but surely), so from a chubby, homely tomboy, I have transformed into a pleasant young woman. I speak about my weight and appearance, because it is the visible symbol of my happiness and my love for Ralph. Before I did not care how I looked. For what? For whom? Now I want to be pretty for Ralph...for me. He gives me the motivation and it is so easy, so satisfying. Thank you, Ralph.

The moral of my story is, that after trying to hide most of the time and being afraid of fully living, I woke up and found the courage to look for my happiness. It was risky, but life rewarded me with a miracle. I want to respect it, not forget about it, work and learn to keep it alive. A man made me a woman. I did not know it, but I was waiting for this.

Everything Happens for the Best

My goal, by telling my story, is to maybe encourage people to not give up their dreams. Life is short. Everyone has the duty to be happy. It is not easy, sometimes, but it is always rewarding to try. It is not just a one-time decision. It is a day-by-day choice. If your life is gratifying, do not forget to realize it everyday. If your life is not satisfying, find a way to improve it, or change it. There is nothing worse than people spending their time complaining how unhappy they are, but not doing anything to correct it.

I am not trying to judge and condemn—even if it seems like it!—I just would like to motivate people to listen to their inner voice and to not be afraid of change.

Life can be a marvelous adventure where, I guarantee you, everything happens for the best.

Postscript

Sam is retired now, resting in Bicycle Heaven. I look at him occasionally, in admiration, and remember the roads we traveled together. He does not know yet, but I am planning a new adventure for us. Some day soon we are going back out on the road, to share our story with the world, to visit people who love bicycles; all kinds of people, and all kinds of bicycles. The bicycle family is so vast and various.

This time our mission is well-defined: encourage other people to follow their dreams, and why not with a bicycle...

Dear Reader,

Thank you for reading my story. I hope that it was entertaining and inspiring.

The fact that you have this book in your hands is another miracle for me.

Like my adventure on bicycle, and my adaptation to a new life, getting this book to you has been a challenge.

I am especially proud of it because when I was in school, I was considered a below-average student. I was even told that I did not have any ability to learn another language.

I know that I am not managing English perfectly, but I keep working on it.

Michelle R. SICARD
Boulevard, California
August 2001

If you have any comments, or questions, I would love to hear from you. You can contact me at any of the following:

⇨ **www.velosam.com**

e⇨ **velosam@earthlink.net**

☎ ⇨ **619-766-4163**

⇨ **P.O. Box 1177**
Boulevard, CA
91905